My Journey up the Mountain.

The Road to Black Belt

Matt Stait

All rights reserved. This book or any portion thereof may not be reproduced or used in any manner whatsoever without the express written permission of the author.

If you would like further information on talks, seminars, or workshops you can connect with me in the following ways:

www.modernsamurai.online

www.modernsamuraiblog.online

www.msma.academy

Facebook

Linkedin

Instagram

CONTENTS

Foreword — 5

Introduction. — 9

Part 1. The search. — 12

    1, Being a kid. — 13

    2, Judo. — 21

    3, Boxing. — 27

    4, Ninja School. — 32

    5, Myth, religion, or martial art? — 37

Part 2. Growing roots. — 41

    6, Meeting a guide on the journey. — 42

    7, When I was a lad, and everything cost 10p. — 47

    8, The fighting jumper. — 51

    9, The paint pot workout. — 58

10, The invisible student.	64
11, How to fail a grading without trying.	69
12, The battle of the big toe.	75

Part 3. Reaching out. 87

13, The end of an era.	88
14, What's in a name?	97
15, Wrestling, but not the Saturday afternoon kind.	102
16, Krav is like a box of chocolates. You never know what you're gonna get. (said in the voice of Forrest Gump).	107
17, There's never a damsel in distress when you need one.	123
18, 'Boing!' said Zebedee.	131
19, A lesson in humility.	136

Part 4. Full circle 141

20, My own place.	142
21, Students.	153
22, Why the doors?	160
23, Teaching security.	167
24, The punch is always the last thing to go.	178
25, What doesn't kill you makes you stronger is bullshit.	183
26, An invite to the dance.	190
27, Why do women shave their eyebrows off only to draw them on again?	197

"It is not the critic who counts; not the man who points out how the strong man stumbles, or where the doer of deeds could have done them better. The credit belongs to the man who is actually in the arena, whose face is marred by dust and sweat and blood; who strives valiantly; who errs, who comes short again and again, because there is no effort without error or shortcoming; but who does actually strive to do the deeds; who knows great enthusiasms, the great devotions, who spends himself in a worthy cause; who at best knows in the end the triumph of high achievement, and who at the worst, if he fails, at least fails while daring greatly, so that his place shall never be with those cold and timid souls who neither know victory or defeat."

Theodore Roosevelt.

FOREWORD

I met Matt in the early summer of 2017 through his work for the anti-violence charity Stand Against Violence. I watched with fascination as he powered through a content-rich, hour-long self-defence taster session with a rapt Year Nine class. The physical side of the lesson was awesome – simple, dynamic and perfectly suited to that age group - but I was equally blown away by Matt's passion for his subject, the intellectual fire behind his presentation, and the way he elicited critical thinking about self-defence from the kids as if it was the most natural thing in the world.

I knew I had to be friends with this person, and two years later I can honestly say that my life is richer for it. Those close to Matt know that he is obsessively, continuously driven to improve himself, and will push you to do the same if you're up for it – challenging your thinking and leaving you inspired, with constant new lines of enquiry to explore.

A few months ago, I described him as a gadfly – an insult famously levelled at Socrates for his tendency to ask provocative, often uncomfortable questions. Matt immediately, gleefully posted this to his Facebook page: *I'm taking this as a compliment of the highest order!*

This book is a vibrant, page-turning recollection of Matt's martial arts journey to date, using the metaphor of a mountain climb. I'm certain Matt hasn't actually reached anything like his summit yet, and his journey will continue onwards and upwards. But midlife (sorry Matt!) is a time when many of us take stock and dive more deeply than ever into what Erik Erikson called "generativity" - the task of passing along the fruits of our learning to others, which in turn enriches our own journey further.

Indeed, mindfulness superstar Jon Kabat-Zinn (JKZ) teaches in *Wherever You Go, There You Are* that coming back down the "mountain" of self-improvement is every bit as important as ascending it:

> *You can't stay at the top of the mountain. The journey up is not complete without the descent, the stepping back and seeing the whole again from afar. Having been at the summit, however, you have gained a new perspective, and it may change your way of seeing forever.*

The image of ongoing ascent and descent runs through *My Journey Up The Mountain*:

> *Many years ago, I was told by one of my instructors that the road to black belt is like climbing a mountain [...] While on the journey it is your responsibility to help others on the path. Those nearer the summit will reach back to offer*

> *support and guidance, those below will reach upwards for that help. We are not alone on this journey and we could not walk it without the help of others. We must respect everyone's individual pathway, as without them we could not grow.*

As with Matt's first book (*Modern Samurai*), this lively collection of stories is underpinned by many deeper themes. In this case, Matt slips a hint into Chapter 5 by hypothesising that martial artists typically live out the so-called "Hero's Journey" blueprint of mythology through their personal stories. Although he doesn't explicitly say it, his own journey as told here mirrors this archetypal pattern beautifully.

In this model, the hero is first called to an adventure. He or she then meets a guide or mentor, and undergoes adventure, transformation and great testing. Finally comes the Return, where as Matt summarises it:

> *This is where we come back to our normal life wiser, stronger and with a new value we bring to the world. For us this could be becoming instructors in our own right and helping others to progress now armed with a skillset and self-belief we previously did not possess. Or a new found sense of worth and ability to overcome adversity.*

Different writers break the journey down into various different sub-stages. Joseph Campbell posits 17 such stages, dubbing the central, pivotal sub-stage: *Atonement with the Father/Abyss*. For example, in

Star Wars, Luke confronts Darth Vader, and then finds that Vader is his father. I won't drop any spoilers into this foreword, but suffice to say that Matt's own experience as an adult of *atonement* with his late father, who he lost as a child, is one of the uncanniest, most moving true stories I've heard for a long time, as well as being a structurally perfect turning point for his life story.

I hope you enjoy this book as much as I did, and are able to apply some of its themes and reflections to your own Hero's Journey - whether that's up the Martial Arts Mountain, or some other terrain which is meaningful to you . . .

Kai Morgan
Martial arts blogger
www.budo-inochi.com
June 2019

INTRODUCTION.

I have just woken up with last night's half-eaten cheese and ham baguette stuck to my face; pushing myself up from the sofa I am greeted with my gi being thrown at me - 'It's 5.45 am; get up!'

Hungover and with a broken big toe I will be expected to complete a six-mile beach run in fifteen minutes as part of my grading . . .

Before I tell my story, I want to make something very clear.

I love martial arts. It has saved me from myself and everything good in my life is as a direct consequence of training.

That being said, amongst the many positive tales there will be stories in the pages and memories that on occasion could show something in a less than positive light. I do not want people to think I am being disrespectful as that is never my intention. I would just like to tell my story openly with both the good and the bad. No edits to appease someone's ego, or rewrites to suit a particular political agenda.

This is just my story and my memories of the arts as they were laid out to me. Not good or bad, better, or worse, but each having its own strengths and beauty that all of us can take something from if we are willing to see past the dogma of style.

Many years ago, I was told by one of my instructors that the road to black belt is like climbing a mountain. There are many paths that lead to the summit and each one is different. While on the journey it is your responsibility to help others on the path. Those nearer the summit will reach back to offer support and guidance, those below will reach upwards for that help. We are not alone on this journey and we could not walk it without the help of others. We must respect everyone's individual pathway, as without them we could not grow.

As the years have gone by, I have seen the truth in this. The students need each other; the instructor needs the student. The instructor needs to remain a student. It is a circle, and each time the summit appears as the clouds break, tantalisingly close, yet just out of reach, we realise there is always more to learn. Each peak opens out to a new vista where more summits rise into a new horizon. There is a wonderful saying that goes:

Sometimes a teacher, always a student.

I have a large tattoo across my back. It is the one you can see on the cover of this book. I have several but this one holds a certain significance. It is a piece of calligraphy of the haiku by Funakoshi Sensei (the founder of modern-day Karate) with the words *Hatsuun jindō,* which translates to: *Parting the clouds, seeking the way.* I think it was around 1994 I had this done as I was immersed in my martial arts journey and the words still hold true today. It remains a constant reminder of that very important part of my personal story.

I do not claim to know everything, and one of the best things about martial arts is that everybody's story is different. I am still on my path; every answer brings a new question, and every new question reminds me there is always more to learn. It is my privilege and honour to have met and trained with some extraordinary people. Please come with me as I introduce a few of them to you.

This is my journey.

PART 1.
THE SEARCH.

The journey of a thousand miles begins with a single step.

Lao Tzu

1, BEING A KID.

My parents had divorced. We had lived in a council house on an estate that was heavily populated with my dad's side of the family. As a kid I don't recall the reasons why the marriage ended other than being witness to a lot of arguing that often turned very unpleasant. The time came for us to move and so we found ourselves in a new area, in a new town with hostility from all sides as we were the new kids with a single mum and no Dad around.

Visits from my Dad were sporadic at best and only made the feeling of isolation worse. I would daydream my way out of the daily misery with the help of Spiderman and Tarzan. At that time these were in my mind the two best heroes ever. I would collect comics and re-enact the scenes within as I jumped from the top of the cupboard to wrestle to the death with the snake-shaped draught excluder that shored up the gap under my seventies bedroom door. As is the way with most young boys I dreamt of facing the world as they did, with no fear.

This book isn't the place to open old wounds so suffice to say my childhood was tough from every angle. Maybe I will write about it one day in a separate piece. I lived in perpetual fear and my daydreams into the world of the superheroes gave me a respite from that. But alas, they were nothing but unobtainable pipe dreams; the odds of my being bitten by a radioactive spider or adopted by a band of gorillas in darkest Africa was pretty much zero, and deep down I knew that.

But then hope arrived, not the impossible superhero kind of the Marvel comics, but real, tangible, and more importantly, attainable. I found martial arts. Here were superpowers that anyone could have if they worked hard enough. No magical spiders or guardian apes required here, just the ability to work hard and dedication. That seemed easy. How wrong I was.

First you had to find a teacher. Back then a black belt was a rare and mythical beast that was spoken of in hushed tones. Clubs were rare and hard to find in small market towns. The search was made even harder by personal circumstances and lack of finances. No matter how hard I looked my Mr Miyagi eluded me. (I had no idea he even existed then, so it is no wonder I couldn't find him).

So, I would watch everything I could, read everything I could get hold of and secretly practise the things I had seen on the Saturday afternoons in front of the TV. As expected, I didn't improve, and my makeshift dojo in the woods did nothing to forward my studies.

On top of that I was forced to move several times over the next few years, each time faced with yet another bunch of irritating in-kids who felt they had to show their superiority by smacking me around. The schools at this time did nothing. In fact I would go so far to say they were complicit as I had my head smashed off a table by my art teacher, was dragged naked through the changing rooms by my hair by the PE teacher and at one point had a stand-up fight with him on the playing fields. As he was one of those rugger bugger types with a serious attitude, he took great delight in punching and kicking me. At probably half his bodyweight it was an unfair match. Every move that I made, every new town and every new school brought with it its own collection of bullies and tormentors. And being the perpetual new kid meant I remained a target throughout those years.

However, I must say at this point, every single bully in my life has gone on to achieve shit. If you are being bullied, please take solace in this.

If you are the bully: Stop it now; you are being a dick and no good will come of it.

One of my favourite memories was accidently bumping into one of my old school bullies one day in a car park. For years he was my nemesis and I would hide from him and his sadistic behaviour. We were both heading the same way, so I followed him through the long alleyway with tall buildings on either side into the main thoroughfare. The whole time he was scared.

We hadn't seen each other in over twenty years but I know that he had heard about my life and what I had become, and he knew it was me. As a child I was nervous and frightened; now I had been a bouncer for many years, fought in a number of competitive styles, held black belts and run a gym. I had learned to control my fear, and as I followed him through the alleyway uncomfortably close on purpose, I smiled to myself as I watched him trying to handle his.

There was no need for me to hit him although I had dreamed of that moment for many years. I often daydreamed of the time I would repay him for the wrongs he caused and the degrading way he treated me. Watching him twitch as I walked behind him, seeing him try to fight his fear as I came close was actually better than battering him. I had won psychologically that day as he had beaten me the same way many years before. It felt strange being so close to someone who once instilled such fear in me, yet I felt nothing but pity for him.

I watched him intently, knowing that my eyes boring into the back of his skull were making him nervous. I was that close he could probably feel my breath; seeing him shrivel before my eyes that day was a sweeter victory than any physical beating. Knowing he was beneath me in every way was the prize. My anger for the wrongs of years gone by faded at the sight of this pathetic man in front of me. Physically there was nothing saying I could not have beaten him, but I didn't. My mind was the weak link and it took me years to see that.

It turns out he was being beaten regularly by his father. He would go home and suffer the wrath of his dad and then try to take it out on anyone he could. A lot of the time that would be me. He was suffering and to make his suffering easier he chose to cause pain to other people. We were just kids and there is no way his juvenile brain had the ability to figure out this kind of problem.

Most, if not all bullies are in reality victims themselves. However, that does not excuse the behaviour or the real harm they cause people. The damage done by bullies is often compounded by the fact that, more often than not, the school or workplace will try to deny its existence as to admit it would reflect badly on them. The repercussions are far reaching, and the consequences can last a lifetime.

I am lucky now that I can help others to stand up to these people. To live a braver life, and gain confidence and physical skills. It gives me amazing satisfaction to help people to step out of the shadows of the bullies and to blossom into the people they should be. Standing up to these bullies and helping others to do so is something I feel very privileged to be able to do and I just wish I could go back in time to speak to my younger self as he ran home from school or hid in the bushes when he heard them coming, and say that one day all this would not matter. If I could just tell him that in time, he would outgrow the little world and those little people, and one day would have this moment in the alleyway.

But alas, I cannot. My younger self never got that message, but I can tell people now. If you are a victim of bullying, if your life is overshadowed by bullying, if you feel there is no escape, trust me there is. I was you once and I know what you are going through. I am not going to say fight back or stand up to them, or any of the other mostly unhelpful phrases you are told. Instead, I am going to say: keep your chin up. It is not your fault and the very things that you are being picked on for will one day make you successful. Your time will come and one day those people you now fear will become the people you use as fuel to create the best life for yourself. Go do what makes you happy and one day you will have your metaphorical moment in the alleyway. One day that bully will shrivel up before your eyes.

My love of martial arts never waned during those times and I watched every movie I could lay my hands on. Bruce Lee and Jackie Chan became my pop stars and I would wade through hundreds of hours of appalling acting and plot just to get those moments where the stars would show us their moves. All the time I was secretly waiting for the day I would find a way to learn.

But it wasn't just the Asian movie stars I followed, I was also a fan of Western films like *No Retreat, No Surrender* with a young Van Damme and of course *The Karate Kid* where Daniel-san gave hope to the nerdy kids across the Western world. He even helped me with my love life would you believe it.

The Betamax vs VHS wars had raged for a number of years and VHS (with the help of porn believe it or not) had won the day. Our local video store was run by a lovely guy who employed an even lovelier girl. She was a few years older than me and very pretty, and she would greet my clumsy flirting with kindness. But apart from that the greatest gift they gave me was to completely ignore the age restrictions on films. They knew I wasn't eighteen, they even knew I wasn't fifteen but still they would let me hire every Kung-fu movie they had in stock and then listen patiently as I enthusiastically critiqued it when I returned the movie to them.

Today was a big day in my world. It was 1984 and *The Karate Kid* was out on video. Today would not be spent self-consciously flirting or spinning the racks of videos searching for a film. Today was all about getting *The Karate Kid*. I was with a mate and we were excited; film in hand we just had to kill some time till his Dad went to work so we could use the TV. On the way back were some tennis courts, and on those courts were some girls we had not seen before. This seemed like a good place to hang out and waste some time. We sat down along the side of the fence and admired the girls playing. One in particular had long bronzed legs, and long curly hair that swayed around as she returned the ball. She was wearing one of those white tennis skirts and bright white shoes. What made her even more alluring was that they were talking to each other in French. I was transfixed.

As they played my friend and I struck up a commentary and were having a lot of fun ad-libbing the game, especially the parts where I would say, '*Sexy Legs is hitting the ball!*' and my mate would reply, '*Nice Tits missed that one!*' In our juvenile minds we were having a great time until the object of my lust stopped the game, marched over and said in a French accent, 'I understand English very well'. Well that spoilt our fun and so we went off to watch the film. We all know how it goes and what an amazing piece of film making it is; we also know that it has stood the test of time and even now it's a film I will revisit every so often.

I felt bad about the girl and the way it was left, and as luck would have it, she was there again when I walked past to return the movie. I gulped in a breath of courage, steeled myself, and with the still fresh memory of Daniel-san getting the girl I marched to the gate at the side of the courts. She saw me and a scowl fell over her pretty face. 'Please,' I shouted. 'Let me apologise for my behaviour yesterday'. She was cautious but allowed me to make my apologies, even agreeing to meet me in fifteen minutes after her game ended. I couldn't believe my luck and nervously sat there counting down the minutes and passing the video box from hand to hand to relieve the tension. When she arrived, she asked what the movie was. When I told her she asked if I knew Karate. 'Not yet,' I replied. 'But I will'. She giggled and we talked.

She was an exchange student and for the rest of her stay we had an innocent teenage romance. On her return to France we became penpals. I would write with all the emotion a teenage heart could muster. But over time the letters got fewer and time between the postman visiting grew, until one day they just stopped altogether. But the promise I made that day was shining more brightly than ever and the frustration of wanting something but having no way to make it happen was beginning to wear me down. Perhaps it was time to forget my silly childhood fantasies. Perhaps it was time to find some new dreams?

2, JUDO.

Punk music was rocking the charts and CB radios were all the rage. I was just a kid.

We had moved to an estate in South Wales; as my parents had recently split up it meant we had to relocate. It was hard being the new kid; skinheads were in fashion and Doc Martens and shaved heads set the scene.

The estate was connected to a large steelworks, and most of the inhabitants worked there. I just remember the eggy smell and the wives rushing out to get the washing in whenever the wind turned in a certain direction. The estate was working class and set aside from everywhere else. Geographically the houses were enclosed by a main road that encircled the entire estate. The buildings were bland and uniform with the small gardens parcelled off where the occupiers had tried to make them their own.

I was having trouble acclimatising to my new world and my mum thought martial arts might be the way. I was a huge fan at this point.

I watched *Kung Fu* with David Carradine as often as I could. Iron Fist on Saturday afternoon wrestling always got my attention, and then Bruce Lee arrived. Here was the answer to my prayers. This was a way for me to rise above the bullies and the misery. Like an entire generation I watched astounded as this guy beat all takers, overcoming amazing odds and doing it all with a certain *joie de vivre* that exuded style, overcoming boundaries like class and race. Here was the hero that we had been waiting for.

My friends of the day and I would leap from sofa to chair, howling as we went in a makeshift attempt to copy the kicks and punches we saw on the screen. We would thumb our noses and beckon our mates forward with an outstretched arm just the same as we had seen Bruce do it.

The first film I saw with Bruce Lee in it was *The Big Boss*. Badly dubbed English that mismatched the movements on the screen finally gave way to the fight scenes. My younger self revelled in them. I did not see the violence before me, just beauty. I knew the blood was fake and the bruises were make-up. It was the movement that drew me. Even then I understood that that was something you could not fake. In a world before CGI and without the obvious wirework of most Chinese films before it the application of the techniques made me gasp in awe. As the film reached its climax in its now iconic scene, I was entranced. Some people feel a passion for football, something I never have, others horse-riding or boating. For me right there, I had found my passion and the fire had been lit.

I was taken to a football game once. My mum had been dating this guy and it was bonding time. The hope I suppose was that we would get to know one another to facilitate Mum's burgeoning relationship. Wasn't going to happen though as I didn't like him and forcing me to watch a football match would only make that worse. But if I thought that would be the end of my misery, I was wrong. It was winter and cold. The air had an evil chill to it that found its way through your clothes and chilled your very core. For some reason the winters back then felt so much bleaker than they do now. Global warming maybe? Or central heating?

My mum had a practical solution to this. She demanded I wear a pair of her tights underneath my trousers. Despite my obvious discomfort and howls of disapproval I was forced to put these on, and we set off with me trying to readjust the gusset with every other step as the tights were riding up my butt. The match was Newport County vs someone, no idea who. I have no idea who won, or the score, or even if the orange silky Newport county scarf I found wrapped around my neck was paid for or not. I had no interest in either the game or my new best pal. My sole concern was not having an accident so the ambulance would not be called, and the paramedics wouldn't have to cut away my trousers to expose the flesh-coloured women's tights that wrinkled around my legs.

From that day to this I have never been to another football game, although I may have worn tights.

My wonder and curiosity for the martial arts however grew, and unlike now where everything is at your fingertips and the Internet shows everything in the moment, the delicious agony of waiting for the next episode of *Kung Fu* or even *Hong Kong Phooey* was a permanent state of being that ebbed and flowed from weekday to weekend as Saturday finally rolled around once again. Only a select few knew of this as the bullies hounded me enough without giving them more ammunition.

On top of that I was a weak kid with asthma. None of the school sports interested me and team exercises of any nature seemed like a pointless waste of time to me. I did not appear at that time like an ideal applicant for a martial arts student. And that was just as well, as coming from a single parent family money to pay for lessons was not something I had.

But finally, I had a chance. Shut away in my room or roaming through the surrounding hills and woods I would spend countless hours alone. Drawing myself further and further away from people, I would have a very select few friends. This has followed me all through my life and although the bullying stopped my need to keep a very small circle has continued. On the estate was a leisure centre; it has since been demolished and is now probably flats or something. In that leisure centre was a Judo class. Back then neither my Mum nor I had any idea of the myriad of styles and systems. It was just martial arts, and I wanted to do it.

I don't remember that much about the first few classes, I turned up in t-shirt and shorts eager to learn but terrified at the same time. The instructor was gruff and when in his gi (the clothing worn for training) he presented an intimidating presence to my younger self. Please remember that at that time I had curly gingery hair and a mass of freckles that clashed with my *Casper the Friendly Ghost* complexion. Top that off with asthma, social anxiety, and hand-me-down second-hand flares and the reality was everything intimidated me.

But I do remember a certain day very well. It has stayed in my head forever and I don't think the instructor even knew just what he did that day and how it affected me. My mum as I have mentioned was a single parent to myself and my sister who is two years younger than me. She also worked full time. Money was incredibly tight but somehow Mum managed to find me a second-hand Judo gi. It came with an orange belt as I assume that is the level the previous owner had graded to. I practised putting it on, fumbling with the belt as I had no idea how to tie one properly.

The day of class came, and I self-consciously stood in the hall with the other kids. The instructor told us to form groups and sit with our ranks. I felt out of place but good. The alien feel of the gi was a distraction, but I looked like everyone else so took comfort in that. I sat with the other beginners, all sporting white belts except me. I knew I wasn't an orange belt, but I couldn't figure out how to keep the gi closed without it and as I didn't own a white belt, I thought it would be ok. The instructor pointed at me and barked that I was in the wrong group. I meekly explained that I was not an orange belt so was in the right group. At that Sensei nearly imploded with indignation. Loudly and in front of all the other kids and parents he demanded I remove the belt at once and I had not earned it and was disrespecting the art by wearing it. I was horrified. All eyes were on me and in that moment, I felt like I had been accused of a great offence. My six-stone self could not find a voice to argue my case. Embarrassed, I removed the belt and slunk off to the corner. Between my shame, and the fact I wasn't going to learn how to do those kicks I coveted so much, I made excuses to avoid going. That was my first experience of the arts and it stopped me from trying another class for quite a long time. I did revisit Judo years later and had a much more positive experience.

3, BOXING.

My second attempt at learning martial arts came courtesy of the local boxing gym. On the estate was a rank of shops set in a square where the old ladies would queue for their pensions and the builders would get a breakfast at the café, and around the back of the shops was a traditional spit and sawdust boxing gym. The place was cramped and smelled of sweat; tatty fight posters were plastered over every spare inch of wall. Bags hung from chains; gaffer tape covered the worst of the wear and tear. I can't remember the trainer's name, but I do remember vividly some important things about my then short-lived boxing career.

The first was the road running. And to make matters worse it wasn't even at a civilised time. No, you were expected to do five to six mile runs at six am in all weathers. The endless slog along the pavements in the grey dawn light was a miserable experience for me. I have never been a fan of either mornings or running, so this was a double kind of hell. I also couldn't get what all the running was for. After all I wanted to learn how to fight so I didn't have to run anymore!

This gym - like a lot of boxing gyms - only took in fighters. You could not go there just to train; if you trained, you fought. Up until that point I had a nice, romanticised version of what sparring would be. I had seen matches on the TV and even seen some boxing films. It is no surprise that the drop-out rate for newcomers is around fifty percent when they spar. I had been training for a few weeks and working on fitness and pad drills. I had diligently done my rounds of skipping and bag work, interspersed with killer circuits of crunches and press-ups. I had even put the road runs in. So, this was it. The moment of truth.

I clumsily pushed down the middle rope with my hand. The gloves I was wearing were borrowed, too big, and ill-fitting. I stepped through the rope and placed my feet on the hallowed ground of the canvas. Around the ring were the trainers and one or two other fighters curious to see the show. In front of me stood a kid similar in size to me but wearing proper boxing boots. My mind fixated on those boots as I didn't have any, and in my head having proper boots meant you must be good. After the *Have a good fight and no dirty stuff* speech from the stand-in ref, the bell was rung, and I moved out towards the centre of the ring and began to circle. My stomach was whirring, my mouth dry, and my muscles felt so cramped it seemed I could barely move.

I saw the punch coming. It's funny how in those moments you can see quite clearly what is happening. My brain was playing catch-up and the internal conversation in my head was giving me the count-down: 'You're being punched'. 'I know,' I replied. 'You better do something'. 'I'm trying,' I told myself. All the while the glove got bigger and bigger as it came towards my face. It appeared like it was coming in slow motion; unfortunately my reactions were even slower. My head snapped back as the jab landed; pain shot through my nose and my eyes started to water. It was the first punch of my first spar, and it hurt!

It is in this moment where your own personal truth comes out. The layers that we wrap ourselves in to cover our vulnerability, and the lies we tell ourselves and others melt away before the onslaught. What happens next and the decision we make tells those who are watching with knowing eyes all they need to know. I remember that day well and over the years I have been witness to many moments like that for many others. It is always a powerful, raw, emotional thing. That first time you are trying to knock out the guy in front of you and he is doing the same for you.

I can't really recall details after that. I could taste blood in my mouth and my lip was already swelling as the final bell rang and I managed to end the round. I was exhausted and my nose throbbed, but underneath all that welled a strange feeling. I couldn't tell if it was excitement or relief, but it felt good. I must have done something right as soon after I was preparing to fight in a show.

I became engulfed in the training; every day I could get there I would. I had to constantly ask myself what I was eating, as making weight was a priority. I remember being shouted at a lot over this period. That fact that I was a kid seemed to be lost and winning was all that mattered. The sparring was ramped up and often I would find myself tumbling to the floor from a hook I hadn't seen, or even worse folding up from the body shot my opponent had just dug into me. Those were the worst and sometimes you would be curled up with tears flowing down your cheeks as the trainer yelled at you to get up. Back then the insults were very sexist and homophobic so I will leave it to your imagination as to the type of abuse I was hearing. Tough love I think they call it!

With the sounds of those voices and the memories of every punch still fresh in my mind, Fight Night had arrived. Something else that sticks in my memory, is that I really didn't like kids' amateur boxing matches back then. Now the safety and care given to the fighters are very different. Rules are in place to protect the kids. It didn't seem that way on this night though.

The venue was a working men's club. The walls and ceiling were nicotine-stained and had that stickiness to them from the years of trapped cigarette smoke. The tables had been arranged around the ring which sat in the middle of the dance floor. Above the ring were some lights and outside the circles of tables sat the bar with its metal pull-down shutters pushed up. Bags of peanuts hung on those cardboard pictures which were placed along the back of the bar next to the optics. Any time anyone brought a bag another portion of a scantily clad woman in a swimsuit would be exposed. Fag machines and one-armed bandits lined the walls. As with most nights a fog of cigarette and cigar smoke drifted above everyone's head as the overweight local businessmen sat at their tables puffing away. They were all in dinner jackets and dickie bows, but not polished in the way you would imagine a black-tie event to be. Each table sent up its own plume as they chattered excitedly and waited to see the upcoming bouts. I remember the air of anticipation that was in the room and it made me uncomfortable.

The fights started and as the night got underway the compère would call the boys up. Red vs blue. We all had vests on with the correct colours. I could hear the cheering and jeering as the fights unfolded in the ring. Finally, it was my turn and I walked towards the steps listening to the announcer say my name. I can't really describe the feeling as it was such a mixed bag of emotions and anyone who has been there will get that. The fight itself was mediocre at best; being honest I can't really remember the fight. It's funny how your mind chooses to remember certain things over others.

What I did remember is feeling uncomfortable seeing grown men get so excited as young boys beat each other. The fervour and pitch of the audience took me back as I could hear the cries of, 'Fuck him up!' and, 'Smash his fucking face in!' that were being yelled towards us. The bloodlust in the crowd overshadowed everything else about that experience for me. I know it is different now and that behaviour would not be tolerated at any decent promotion, but the world back then had different standards than it does now.

And yet again no kicks. The thing I wanted to learn above all else back then.

So once again my journey into the martial arts faltered.

4, NINJA SCHOOL.

The eighties had rolled around and with it a shift in fashion. Now Ninja movies were all the rage, and if you didn't have ninjas in your show, well, it wasn't worth watching.

Ninjas, for those that don't know come from a secretive world. Trained assassins famed for their skill and lack of emotion. Clad head to toe in black, with a mask to disguise their features, they would use the cover of night to silently dispatch the intended target with calculated precision.

If memory serves me right, they were subdivided into *ryū* or clans. Each specialised in a certain area. They were known not just for their use of weapons, but also poisons and subterfuge.

There is a story people tell about a hired ninja assassin. I have no idea if it is true, but it certainly highlights the mindset of the ninja.

Once there was a feudal lord. He was a very wealthy man that lived in a palace surrounded by guards. He rarely left his home which was high on a hill surrounded by walls just as high, with large imposing gates that were manned at all times by the palace guard. The guard also patrolled the walls; armed and well trained, they were a fighting force to be reckoned with. But the lord also had an inner defence. Constantly in his presence were the personal guard. A dozen highly skilled and seasoned warriors. Each chosen for his ability in battle with proven loyalty to the lord. Each of these men would die to save his life.

The lord being rich and powerful had equally rich and powerful enemies and they conspired against him. Numerous attempts had been made on his life, and all had failed. So, it was at this point that his enemies hired a ninja!

Ninjas were more than just cold-blooded murderers; they were highly skilled in all aspects of death. He knew he could not just rush in and overpower all the guards using violence, so he had to find another way. For a few days the ninja gathered information and probed for weaknesses in the routine of the guard. He was looking for an in, a way for him to reach the lord undetected. It was also imperative that he had a valid escape plan in place so once the deed was done, he could make his getaway before anyone knew something was up. Over time the unnamed man formulated a plan.

It was in the small hours before the dawn, when everything is still, that the ninja quietly slipped out of the building. Checking to make sure no one was watching he made his way to the palace, where he had found a guard he could bribe to let him in. He snuck down the alleyways, between the houses; nothing more than a passing shadow, until he finally made it to the lord's private residence. Being very careful not to alert the guards he made his way to the latrine. Toilets in those times were nothing more than large holes in the ground. You would sit over the hole and relieve yourself as the empty space slowly filled with waste. This was where the ninja had chosen to wait. Under the cover of darkness, he had made his way to the hole. Trying not to focus on the stench, he slowly sank into the ooze and started to prepare.

Every morning the lord would perform his routine. He would toilet and bathe before going to breakfast. Staff would lay out towels and his clothes for the day. The ninja knew this and patiently waited as the sun started to peek over the horizon and slowly rise.

The lord entered the toilet, adjusted himself and sat down. Instantly he felt a sharp pain. Very quickly he began to feel dizzy and light-headed. Seconds later he slumped to the floor dead. The ninja had been in position for this moment, so as the bare arse of the lord squatted down, he sucked in a quick breath and then blew. The breath entered the blowpipe propelling the dart up and into the corpulent backside of the master. The poison that had been applied to the tip of the dart quickly entered the bloodstream and coursed through his veins. In less than ten seconds the lord was dead.

Silently the ninja collected his things and removed the dart. The only evidence of foul play was a tiny pinprick where the dart had embedded into flesh. Almost unnoticeable to the naked eye, he then crawled out from the human waste that he had sat in for hours and made his escape. No one saw him.

Feudal Japan was a long time ago and far away, but it seemed the skills had travelled across both time and space, as here I was in another leisure centre in another small town about to try a class in Ninjutsu. I had seen the poster in the paper shop window. It had a picture of a figure clad in black, wearing ninja shoes. The ones with the dividers between the big toe and the others. In his one hand was a Katana raised in a killing blow. Shuriken (throwing stars) were drawn in an attempt to make it look as if they were flying off the poster. I can't remember the exact wording, but it went something like:

Learn the deadly secrets of the ninja.

And I did want to learn. Which is why I had made my way to the leisure centre. I was alone and nervous and so instead of going into the class I hung around the snack machines procrastinating over a Wham bar or just manning up and going in. I had seen others make their way into the hall and my mental tug of war was having a right laugh at my expense. I could hear a loud voice shouting; the chattering stopped, which I assumed meant the start of the class, so I forced myself to go through the door. I sort of sidled in and slid along the wall to a nearby folding seat where I quickly sat hoping that no one had seen my entrance.

It was at that moment that I was actually pleased my procrastination had kept me from being on time. Running around the hall on tiptoe in an almost cartoonish fashion were twelve or thirteen people. They were all following a short, rotund guy who was shouting out that this was *ninja running*. If you have ever seen that wildlife clip with the lizard hopping from one foot to the other on the hot sand, he was a cross between that and the Michelin man in black. He had on the outfit without the mask which pulled tight across his gut; short legs waddled under him as he pumped his knees up and down while remaining on the tips of his toes. The whole scene looked absurd to my young eyes and in no way seemed to represent anything even close to deadly. So, with a disappointed sigh I snuck out the way I had come in and once again told myself maybe it just wasn't meant to be.

I just want to add a quick note to this. Many years later I met a guy who said he was a 4th dan in Ninjutsu and he had some real, genuine skills.

5, MYTH, RELIGION, OR MARTIAL ART?

When it comes to martial arts and the students that practise it, I think we have far more in common than we do things that separate us. Martial arts fulfil something within us, and for some of us have become a lifelong pursuit. When talking to others about training the majority reach immediately to the physical side of what we do. They are quick to see the punches, kicks, throws and takedowns but often don't realise that that is just the medium we have chosen to try to harness our minds. It is the conduit we use to develop our physical and mental selves and hopefully reach the best version of us we can be.

Ask yourself what was it you were searching for when you started training? What were you hoping to gain from the constant practice and repetition? Some will say fitness or to defend themselves. Maybe even to lose weight. I would counter and say: look deeper; those are the superficial reasons you tell yourself to get you through the door and to shield you from the level of self-awareness needed to see past that. I am not suggesting this is true for everybody as the number of people who fall along the wayside is many, and a hundred are lost for every one that manages even the first few steps. But that one, the one who sticks with it and stays on the path, has a deeper reason and if you are one of those few reading this you will understand.

There is a concept in mythology known as the Hero's Journey. It sets out a set of steps taken on that journey, and was popularised by Joseph Campbell who leaned heavily on Carl Jung's view on mythology. If you look at almost any story from *Star Wars* to *Kickboxer*, it follows the same general pattern. What's interesting is that this journey is remarkably similar to the journey through the martial arts. Perhaps this is the need within us. Perhaps this is what drives us to keep striving. Perhaps we all really do want to be the hero in our own movie.

The basic premise is that the journey has three main stages:

1. Departure.

2. Initiation.

3. Return.

At the start you are called to an adventure.

For us this would be joining a class and taking those first steps towards becoming a Black Belt.

In *Star Wars* it was Luke Skywalker losing his family and planet, forcing him to try to find Obi-wan.

We then must meet a mentor.

Your Sensei, Sifu, master or coach becomes that person; we look to follow their guidance and leadership and place ourselves in their hands.

In the movie it's the famous little green guy Yoda. 'There is no try, only do'. I guarantee you said that in your head in the Yoda voice.

Next is the transformation.

For us it would be the progression through the ranking system, or competitions won, or forms mastered. Every new colour, accolade or grade opens up a new level to manoeuvre through and another level of self-mastery to overcome.

For Luke it was learning to use the force.

Then would come the Abyss. A test of great magnitude.

For us I suppose we could simplify it and suggest that your black belt exam will be or was that test. It may be however, that your personal test lies elsewhere. Maybe a championship competition or something in your professional life.

For Luke in the finale of the film he faced his nemesis Darth Vader, and (spoiler alert) found out that he was his real father.

Finally comes the Return.

This is where we come back to our normal life wiser, stronger and with a new value we bring to the world.

For us this could be becoming instructors in our own right and helping others to progress now armed with a skillset and self-belief we previously did not possess. Or a newfound sense of worth and ability to overcome adversity.

For Luke it meant helping to overthrow the empire and bring peace to the galaxy.

PART 2.
GROWING ROOTS.

It is not the beauty of a building you should look at; it's the construction of the foundation that will stand the test of time.

David Allen Coe.

6, MEETING A GUIDE ON THE JOURNEY.

Mentors and guides don't always need to be black belts and instructors; sometimes they can be a person just a step or two ahead of you.

I had moved across town and we had ourselves a really nice flat in one of the better areas. It was a fresh start and an opportunity to follow my dreams. I had passed a Karate dojo earlier in the day. It was a converted church with large red wooden doors that opened inward. The club has a few parking spaces outside and an old stone step at the bottom of the doorway. I have sat on that step many times over the years, but for now it was the entrance to a secret world of wonders yet to be discovered.

But first let me paint you a picture of me at that time. I was a young man with long hair that reached down my back in dark curly waves. I wore earrings and cowboy boots and for a while sang in bands on and off. I was tall and gangly with a pigeon chest; freckles stood out against my pale skin. I had always had anger issues and was socially awkward. This was compounded by looking like this with a Welsh accent in Bristol. Once again, I was going to step back into martial arts.

The club I had seen taught traditional Wadō-ryū karate and it was headed by a short powerful man with a ready smile and kind eyes. I was lucky enough on occasion to catch sight of him performing Kata (the sequences of choreographed moves called patterns within the system). His movement was both fluid and sharp; he would slide across the floor and then snap out the strike with precision and focus. The beauty of the movement of Karate kata is to my mind akin to art. I never really mastered it and found it at the time complicated and frustrating. As a young man I just wanted to hit things. I didn't know enough then to see the value it offered. But to this day it speaks to me when I see it done well.

The head of the club at the time was a 6th dan and Sensei had achieved the rank of 1st dan black belt the year I was born. I had no idea of the quality of knowledge that was in that building when I first went there, and it was those years training in that converted church that built the foundations for all that was to follow. Without the help and guidance of all the wonderful instructors and fellow students I met I would not be here writing this today.

It is not an over-exaggeration to say that this club and the people in it changed my life.

I approached the big, red doors and stood there as my heart pounded. Coming from inside I could hear things being hit and loud shouts. I later learned that the thuds of impact were knuckles connecting to the *Makiwara* and the yells were the focused *Kiai* of the Karateka as they practised. The doors were closed but the timetable stuck on the wall said they were open, so I took a deep breath, reached a foot forward, placed it on that step for the very first time, and knocked on the door.

I waited for what seemed like an eternity as I fought the overwhelming urge to just turn around and walk away. I remember this moment whenever a new student comes to my gym as it is a big step with untold possibilities ahead. Finally, the door opened, and a man stood before me. He was balding and had shaved the rest close to match. He stood around six foot one with strong powerful shoulders attached to large forearms, with old faded tattoos on them that led to big meaty calloused hands. They were the hands of a working man, scarred and leathery topped off with the enlarged front two knuckles from constantly striking. He was wearing a slightly faded gi, the white a little dull. His exposed chest showed curly greying hair and droplets of sweat clung to his forehead. Around his waist was a green belt and as he looked at me, he smiled and said hello showing imperfect teeth and a Bristolian accent. His name was Chris and he ushered me in.

As I walked through those hallowed doors for the first time it was like a sensory overload. The first thing was the smell; it was the smell of sweat, hard work and determination with the faintest hint of bleach. This is a smell I have come to savour over the years and no matter where I am if I can smell that smell I feel like I am home. This is exactly what a Dojo should smell like. As I stood in the passage, I could see the matted area through the doorway where rows of students in white gi were punching the air in a low stance while Sensei shouted, 'Ichi, Ni,' which translates as 'One, Two,' in English.

The mats were a light greenish colour and the room was quite small. The walls were sectioned off in little wooden squares with the centres painted white. Mats reached halfway up the walls and also encased the pillars on either side. Those pillars had been used for punching practice and the mats had holes worn into them from the years of repetition. In the alcoves along the walls were trophies and medals from competitions that the club had won. Along the back wall where Sensei stood were mirrors along a section of the wall. A small raised platform area had more mirrors and a mini shrine with a picture of Otsuka Sensei accompanying it. We would bow to his likeness at the start and end of every lesson. There would be three bows. We would stand and then kneel in a very formal manner, left knee first followed by the right. You would then sit back on your ankles, back straight with toes flat and hands on your thighs. Sensei would then shout, 'Rei!' and you would bow once to Otsuka Sensei. On the second 'Rei' we would bow to the Sensei taking the class and on the third we would bow to our fellow students. We never started or finished a class without this.

Chris was grinning at me as I took all this in with eyes wide. It looked just like a movie set, and when he told me to put my things in the changing room I snapped out of my torpor and hurried to do what he asked. Shoes off and ill-fitting jogging bottoms on I went to step through the doorway onto the mats. Chris blocked my path with his hand and explained I had to bow on entering and leaving the training area. So much etiquette to learn and I really didn't want to screw up and offend anyone. I bowed my way in, imitating the exact movement I had been shown and took my place at the end of the furthest line. This was the first Karate class I ever took, and Chris became a friend and mentor to me during this time. I had been given the gift of a Sempai, sometimes referred to as an older brother, but essentially a higher graded student than you who takes you under their wing. One of the things I remember vividly is the day I passed my own green belt grading and Chris bestowed upon me his green belt for me to wear. It was an honour for me to accept it and as it was the first Karate belt I had ever seen, its significance was even more special.

7, WHEN I WAS A LAD, AND EVERYTHING COST 10P.

If you are reading these pages and you are under thirty-five you will recoil in horror at what I am about to say. There is a good chance you will be shaking your head in utter disbelief that people could live such an existence. I am talking about a world before the Internet.

I had been training in earnest for my upcoming grading. Every Saturday morning at ten I had private tuition from my Sensei where I would be left breathless and sweaty from the repetitions of Kata. Our small group of Karateka would also supplement regular classes with 6.30am meets on the famous Clifton Down where we would run around the perimeter and hang punch bags in the trees. Then we would head off to work, but the training didn't stop there.

At the time I was working as a price work decorator on building sites. The more you did the more money you could earn, so that meant that I would walk into a new build property and spend a week or more painting the whole thing ready for its new occupants to come in and redecorate to their tastes. The work was dirty and hard, the pace had to be quick to make money and so our breaks were short. Lunchtime would see me going off alone to find an empty room. I would use paint pots in a DIY version of kettlebells and practise high kicks in my heavy work boots. Every spare minute was utilised in trying to perfect my physical Karate. I will talk about this type of training further on in the book.

As the grading loomed ever closer the thing that was haunting me most of all was the language. All commands on the day of the test would be in Japanese. A panel of highly graded Sensei would sit at a table. Stiff and formal they would call you out and then bark the techniques at you. It is not a place for those with a flighty disposition and standing on those mats having every movement scrutinised by people you one day aspire to be like is truly nerve-racking.

At that time, we were a tight little band of students. We had a few who were of similar grades, so we naturally bonded together. Again, it highlights just how great martial arts are for bringing people together, as in the group were a doctor, a solicitor, an accountant, an electrician, a carpet fitter, a musician and me. What's also interesting is that out of our group almost all dropped out around green belt, and none made it further than brown. I am the sole survivor, which shows the attrition rates back then.

One of the guys was called Rich. He was a slight, softly-spoken guy with a huge intellect and very caring heart. He was a vegan back when very few people knew of the lifestyle, and would never force his views onto others unlike some of the more militant of that fraternity today. He worked for an accountancy firm and was rewarded handsomely for his skills with the salary he commanded. It was almost as if we were polar opposites in many ways. I worked on a building site and am a physical being. I could not be confined to a desk and was very sure in my prowess and abilities. But they say opposites attract and we became good friends through training and would often work out together and sit back after classes to discuss all things martial. I liked the way he challenged me to look at the mental aspects of training; he would always see a deeper meaning to everything, and it was the perfect yin to my yang to counterbalance my superficial physical thoughts.

As he worked from a platform of a good education and knew how to learn, I found him to be the perfect partner in our attempts to learn such an alien language. Japanese is not like European languages where there is a commonality to the structure. Sometimes with French or Spanish the familiar is comforting even if you don't quite grasp the meaning. Not so with Japanese. Nothing in it is anything like English. There are no sounds similar enough to hook your fingers onto, and when written it becomes hieroglyphics into the unknown. We were not learning the whole language, thank goodness. But we did need to know all of our techniques and combinations; we also needed to understand the etiquette and polite phrases as some of our instructors were Japanese and expected courtesy and respect from all students. As an aside I had to do the same thing but with Korean when grading in Tae Kwon Do years later.

Now, we would just reach for our smartphones and translate it, but back then they didn't exist. None of us had a mobile phone, Google was an impossible dream; we had to physically go to the library and hope they would have a text to answer our questions. But we did have our version of cutting-edge technology. It was called a cassette recorder.

We had a handheld flat tape deck with a flip door on the top that opened to allow the tapes to be inserted and a row of big chunky buttons along the front. Above the last switch in the row was a red circle; this was the record button and you would hold it down along with the play button while you spoke into it. Both Richard and I would hold our grading books with the translations written down and try to form the sounds as we had heard them into the speaker. Hunched on the floor of his flat we would sit on the carpet leaning over the device while we tried to enunciate clearly, overly exaggerating the mouth shapes just as a singer would do for their warm-up exercises. We would record the techniques in Japanese and then repeat them in English. We would then play the cassettes in the car and on our Walkmans, in fact everywhere we went. The grading became an obsession and I was not going to fail because I did not know the words.

8, THE FIGHTING JUMPER.

The year was '92 maybe '93, I was in my early twenties and filling my boots. By this stage I was a brown belt in Karate and stood six two with a number of competition wins to my name. My muscles rippled under my skin when I moved, and not an ounce of fat was to be found. My ego and sense of self- importance reigned supreme and the energy I was giving out to the world at this point was narcissistic and self-absorbed. None of this was the fault of my sensei; I was just young with a vitality that was overflowing and carrying the chip on every young man's shoulder as I wanted the world to recognise my worth.

Physically I was strong as a bull, blessed with a body that could perform the tasks asked; mentally I was weak as I struggled to see the deeper meanings of the practice. My instructors saw my struggle and tried to help me to follow the right path.

Over time I received a number of items of clothing from the club. One of the gifts was a tie pin. Made of metal, the small, round pin depicted the symbol of our art: a fist surrounded by the wings of a dove. The style created by Otsuka was one of the five main styles of Karate and the dove held equal relevance to the fist. I was told at the time of receiving the pin that only black belts were given one. I still own the pin to this day; it stays safely locked away so I can occasionally open the box and reminisce about those times I am so grateful for.

The second item was a gift given to me by my sensei. A few other students and I had taken it upon ourselves to start a study group in the mornings before our working day started. Our select few would meet on Clifton Down at six am. Cars would pull up and plumes of hot air from our mouths would condense on meeting the chill of the morning sun as we greeted one another. We would look to run a lap or two of the downs, shadowboxing as we went. I am sure I was not the only one to play the *Rocky* theme tune in my head. Run done we would open the boot of the car and pull out the tatty punchbag. It was a hand-me-down of dubious origin that was probably more tape than bag, but it inspired a reverence in us akin to a religious artefact. Like a lot of traditional dojos ours did not have hanging bags so this was an indulgence for our group. It would be hung from a convenient tree where we would enthusiastically punch and kick it as the early morning dog walkers and joggers went by muttering at us under their breath. After the bagwork we would put on our sparring mitts and work some rounds, looking completely out of place to the commuters walking past.

This diligence in our training earned us a call from Sensei to meet him upstairs. We were greeted at the top with a small pile of jackets, all proudly displaying the insignia of the club. Sensei told us it was his gift to us in recognition of the work we were putting in. Only a few of us received them and my chest swelled with pride to be rewarded in such a manner. They were blue and lightweight in a casual raincoat fashion. They may have only cost a few pounds to print but they were priceless to us and to this day remain one of my fondest remembered gifts as that jacket signified a turning point in my training.

The final piece of clothing and the title of this chapter was something I bought from the club. It was a jumper or more precisely a sweatshirt. It was cream and had the style's logo on the left breast. One of the most amazing qualities of this particular piece of clothing was that it would attract trouble whenever I wore it. How much of that attraction was me I don't know, but the jumper compounded and amplified any signal I was transmitting, and confrontation quickly followed.

It quickly became a standing joke that to wear it was to invite trouble. It was like a beacon to troublemakers, drawing them in as a moth is drawn to the light. Phrases like, 'Do you think you're hard mate?' and, 'Judo would kick your arse,' were flung at me by random passers-by with alarming regularity. Random though, is perhaps not the right word. I was never asked these questions by women, or men over forty. It was always by young capable guys who decided that my jumper was a direct insult to their very existence.

I was sat in a bar one day with a mate; it was around late afternoon on a sunny Saturday when the door swung wide and in marched an older man with a young man swaggering in tow. The older man announced that the young man was the hardest man in Ireland apparently and would fight anyone in the bar right here, right now. They were from the travelling community and the thick accent did nothing to disguise the words that had been launched like missiles to broadside the bar's inhabitants. It was as if every male in the room had suddenly dropped a contact lens; feet shuffled, and all eyes stared at the floor like a goth disco. 'Who will have the crack?' the older man asked moving from man to man and getting uncomfortably close, making them step back and concede space. It was a masterclass in arrogance, and no one was going to take the bait.

My friend who was ex-military and a boxer and no slouch himself looked at me and raised his eyebrows. He then whispered that perhaps I should put my jacket on over my jumper. As luck would have it, I was wearing that jumper, the fighting one, and sure enough the gaze of the older man fell towards the table where we were sat. 'What about you big fella?' he said pointing at me. 'I will put a hundred pounds down that you can't beat my man'. The bar turned to look at me while I weighed up what was happening. Firstly, I didn't have one hundred pounds, secondly my bare-knuckle boxing skills were up there with my ability to fly a frog or turn water into wine. As a martial artist I preferred my violence a little more sanitised back then. Fortunately, my prowess was not tested that day as at that point two coppers came in and after a quick heated debate the travellers left the bar. The landlord it seems had called for backup rather than have bloodshed in his pub. I jokingly told my mate he got off lightly, but we both knew back then I would have almost certainly lost my hundred quid if he really had been the hardest man in Ireland.

Many years ago, I enjoyed a game of pool and sometimes would play for various pub teams. This particular pub was a small local place set in a working men's area of Bristol where villains and rough men would meet. The place was friendly in a hard, no-nonsense kind of way and the social etiquette of the bar was not written down but rigidly enforced. I once passed three guys kicking lumps out of a guy on the pavement directly outside on my way to the bar. As I got closer, they looked up from the task at hand and greeted me, telling me, 'This nonce has just got done for messing with kids'. I sidestepped around the prone man and entered the bar. The locals were lined up on stools, beverage of choice in hand, watching the show through the sign-written windows as if it were a film on a giant plasma TV screen. The occasional *Ooh!* could be heard as boot met body, as the local vigilante justice was being meted out.

This was the bar I was now at and I was there with the team ready for tonight's league game. The opposing team were heading to us from another bar across town. The away players headed in and started ordering drinks before trying to get a warm-up in ahead of the game starting. As always people were weighing each other up and one lad in particular was giving me an awful lot of attention. I assessed him from my stool and noticed the calloused scar tissue around his eyebrows and the nose flattened from many rounds in the ring. He had a hard, wiry body and moved well. I had no need to ask; he was a boxer and he had seen my jumper. Why oh why did I not learn? Why wear the bloody thing to bars, knowing the reaction it created? Tonight was no different.

It didn't take long for Boxer Boy to instigate a conversation. He shoehorned his love of boxing into the conversation as a militant vegan or religious zealot will. I waited, not taking the bait, knowing what was to come. And there it was. 'I reckon boxing's better than Karate mate; what do you think?' The question is never asked in pursuit of knowledge, more as a prelude to confrontation. Just as two lovers will engage in foreplay to heighten and stimulate the senses, the boxer was trying to get me in the mood. So, the dance began.

We chatted for a bit in a slightly barbed way while he metaphorically jabbed me with loaded questions. I parried with my answers and using topic changes as footwork tried to dance around him. All the while he was trying to close down the ring and box me into a corner. I would counter his comment with one of my own as he probed for weakness, looking for the chink in my armour where I would either capitulate or confront. He was spoiling for a fight and I knew it. Not wanting to have to take that route, but also unable to back down in my own ego-fuelled mind I had to find a solution or get into a row. I took stock of the situation and visualised double legging him to the ground and then choking him out. I wanted no part of a stand-up striking fight with him, so the plan was to overwhelm and drag his arse to the floor if it came to that.

Luckily I had boxed as an amateur (badly) and at that time was training a student privately at one of the more famous boxing gyms in the area for an unlicensed fight, so I knew a few names to drop into the conversation while making it clear through my tone and body language that if I had to I would. Turns out we knew quite a few of the same people and the prickliness dissipated with a new-found camaraderie.

I gave him my honest opinion at that time on the question, now we were on firmer ground with regards to what he asked. I explained how there are good and bad examples of everything but in my humble opinion the striking of boxing is far superior to the linear punches from the waist of traditional Karate. Also, that the live training of boxing with the endless rounds and bagwork created much better movement compared to the static lines of Karateka punching air in a one-size-fits-all fashion. I then went on to explain that although boxing was the clear winner in that sense, it had no kicks, throws, locks or ground game. That coupled with the fact it is a sport hampered by rules evened the odds a little. He could see the rationale of the argument and we parted company having reached the conclusion that boxing just snuck the lead in our game of top trumps as it was practised with contact and intent, something rarely done in the majority of dojos.

I bumped into the same guy years later. He reminded me of the conversation and claimed that he was glad we never got to find out which was better, as knowing all about me now he was sure he would have lost. I appreciated the sentiment, but I am fully aware he was being polite as his own record in the ring in the passing years had been impressive.

9, THE PAINT POT WORKOUT.

I was on a building site in Cheltenham. The safety helmet I now wore had a sticker on with the date biroed in; this was to show I had done the tedious and utterly pointless safety induction for the site. Questions like: 'If you saw a hole in the road would you A: jump it, B: walk around it or C: fall in it?' and, 'What is the purpose of safety footwear?' These were always run by some twelve-year-old university student who couldn't build anything with his own hands even if you gave the fella a Lego set.

As I said earlier, I was a self-employed price work painter; this basically translated to: don't be sick as you get nothing; don't take breaks as you're not paid for them; don't even think about slowing down as you get paid per unit; and if it takes a week or a month to finish the house you still get exactly the same. Speed was the name of the game, and as we were always right up the arse of the other trades to get it finished, occasionally tensions would rise.

These were new build houses; brand new estates full of soulless buildings with paper-thin walls surrounded by many others in the same style. The only differences would be the number of bedrooms and ensuites each had. That was the one-upmanship of the buyers to get as many bathrooms as their mortgage would allow. We would traipse through the mud to get to them as usually the connecting roads had yet to be laid, and once there we would bang on the radio and get to it.

As *Classic Gold* echoed round the empty rooms my partner and I would sing along badly to the hits of the sixties through eighties while we started the process of decorating the house. At this point everything was bare. Plasterboard and doorframes lay exposed and often unfinished, the bare wood showing the capabilities of the carpenter that fitted them. It turns out that not all carpenters are created equal and some were blatantly better than others.

The houses would almost always be finished to the exact same specifications: magnolia walls and white gloss woodwork. Day after day, week after week and year after year I would arrive at sites up and down the country, and sell my life in exchange for painting homes I could never afford to buy on the money I received. But I was fit and strong and the work although dirty and back-breaking did pay for my martial arts journey to continue. The fact I was self-employed meant that when a competition, seminar or weekend course came up I didn't need to ask my boss for the time off and pray that he would say yes; I could just go. That was important to me as martial arts were my number one priority.

I had been offered the opportunity to represent England and compete in Switzerland so I was training as hard as I could and any opportunity to squeeze in a little more training was seized with both hands. My routine during those days was pretty simple. The ten o'clock tea break would see me poring over the latest edition of *Martial Arts Illustrated*, *Combat Magazine* and *Inside Karate*. This was long before the days of the Internet, and Bob Sykes and Paul Clifton as editors of these publications were the keepers of the keys to the window through which I saw this world. Religiously I would flick through the pages, hungrily devouring every morsel of martial information I could. I would turn the magazines this way and that trying to decipher the techniques in the photo tutorials as they would give you a step-by-step guide. Legends of the day would grace the covers and in-depth interviews and columns by martial artists from all walks would share their wisdom with us. I like many others owe a huge debt to these men and women for helping to make all this knowledge accessible and to be part of my journey. It has been my good fortune to have met, trained, and worked alongside many of these great people as the years have gone on. I have even had the honour to have written for the updated version of *Martial Arts Illustrated*.

Break over we would get back to work and continue the conveyer belt process of transforming the empty shell to a habitable home. First would be a mist coat. We would arm ourselves with large twelve-inch rollers on poles and work from the top of the house to the bottom rolling in all the walls. Next, we would cut everything in, working fast and kicking along a hop-up stool to reach the ceiling lines. The ceilings would be brought in and rolled, which would leave the back muscles aching after doing the entire house. Woodwork would be primed, filled, and sanded down. An entire morning would be dedicated to caulking up all the gaps. Caulk is flexible filler that comes in a tube; think like a giant tube of toothpaste. This would be placed in a gun and we would crawl around filling all the skirting lines and doorframe edges. You would pipe a line along the gap, wet your finger with spit and run it along to smooth it out. I wish the caulk had been more like toothpaste though, as it tasted horrible and a minty tang would have been a welcome change. After the morning the tip of your index finger would be raw and sore, but no rest was allowed as now all the walls needed prepping and painting.

Once the walls had received their finish coat and all the undercoating had been done it was time to do the glossing. Oil-based paints are no good for the lungs, but we couldn't open the windows as the breeze would blow the building site dust onto the paintwork. So, for two days we would shut all doors and windows and lock ourselves into a house that was full of chemical fumes. The doors would be tackled in one go. A small rad roller and tray would be accompanied by a good quality gloss brush and with a practised hand the full door could be finished in around fifteen minutes. Skirtings came last and crawling along the uncarpeted floor offered no mercy to either your back or knees. The whites or overalls we wore as our painters' uniform often came with knee padding built in, but this would never stay in place underneath you. It was a harsh, difficult, and physically demanding process, but it was one I repeated thousands of times at substantial cost to my body.

Lunchtime would come around and with the vitality of youth and an enthusiasm akin to a Labrador puppy I would shoot off to find an empty room away from the lads eating their sandwiches while chatting about football and which Page 3 girl they would give one to. I had no fancy equipment but would use this time to get in another workout and work on my martial arts.

One of the things I would use was paint pots. I have found the explosion of kettlebell workouts very interesting as I was doing similar things with my paint tins long before they were fashionable. I don't pretend to have invented the workouts though, and hold my hands up to stealing or borrowing a lot of concepts from Gōjū Ryū style training with the clubs and pots. I would lift and swing the tins in ways designed to aid my overall strength. Versions of Turkish get ups and Sumo squats would be interspersed with explosive press ups and burpees. Nothing grand but here's a truth the majority of the fitness industry don't want you to know. You don't need expensive equipment or a twelve-month gym membership or even branded action leggings. You can get a full body workout using the simplest of items.

I would always try to incorporate some sort of martial benefit to the things I did, so unloading the large plastic tubs of emulsion paint from the delivery truck and carrying them to the house became my version of a farmers' walk. I would load two in each hand and start the slow walk towards our plot. As I got closer my grip would start to falter and my back and shoulder muscles would start to really burn, but each step was a step where I was being paid to do my training and each step was making me a better Karateka. Cutting in ceiling lines was something I would relish as it would mean I would have to step up onto my hop- up platform repeatedly. Every time I performed the action was one more rep accomplished. People spend hard cash on classes where they step on and off a raised platform to music, and here I was getting paid to do the same thing. Clambering up ladders was enthusiastically tackled as were flights of stairs. If I had to carry pots of paints with me then all the better. Sod Daniel-san and his pathetic *wax on and wax off*; this was really putting work to work for me. Every physical movement became extra training and any and all jobs translated to exercises I could use to improve.

10, THE INVISIBLE STUDENT.

It's interesting but in the Japanese culture people don't like to scream and shout. You must master your emotions and not make a scene. The Eastern answer to a problem is just to ignore it until it goes away and the same could be said for students. Break the rules or show you are not worthy of their time and you will be gently admonished; repeat the action and you risk becoming a ghost. One of the nowhere students that exist on another plane, drifting from class to class, invisible to the sensei until one day they disappear for good. They either move somewhere else to practise, or more commonly quit Karate and tell people at dinner parties they used to do a bit of martial arts.

These lost souls are the products of their own actions, as we start as a blank slate. When we first step onto the mats we are a nothing. Yes, we exist, but we have not existed in this world. From that moment our actions, thoughts and deeds determine how we are treated. Are we lazy, hot-headed, or self-centred? Do we have a taste for hurting people, or are we crippled by doubt? All our traits and flaws are exposed and laid bare on those mats through correct training. All the things we try to hide become glaringly obvious as we are pushed mentally and physically - well beyond what we thought we were capable of.

If a student is found wanting or is not giving the proper effort they will be encouraged and motivated. If they cannot or will not do what is needed, then eventually they will slip into this limbo existence. Allowed to train, but no one will freely waste energy or time on them. You can make it back from this, but it is a tough slog and many hardships will need to be endured. The world is a different place now so maybe it's different in many modern clubs, but it was a lesson I learned a long time ago and it stays with me.

It was a tough period for me; my personal demons were shouting loudly, and bad habits were taking root. Back then I had a private session with one of my sensei every Saturday morning at ten am. I had been progressing well and was a well-established member of the club. Unfortunately, the other side of me was drawn to the lights and noise of the big city nightlife, and back then crawling home at four am was not unusual. I would often turn up for these lessons sweating what felt like pure alcohol with barely a few hours' sleep. I would stink of beer and the sweat would soak my gi in minutes.

It was a strange time as I was leading this dual life not unlike some perverse comic book superhero character. By day dedicated karateka and willing student dedicated to training and doing all the right things, but as night fell the dark in me would well up and whisper in my ear. All the good in the day was undone in a whirl of partying and booze where I would become this hedonistic monster on a self-gratifying downward spiral that would invariably end with me broke and hungover. This was one of the main motivators to do the doors and work security. At least that way I was getting paid to be out all hours.

My sensei could see this and knew what was happening. The smell of fags, booze, and cheap perfume would cling to me no matter how clean my gi was, and the cracks were starting to show. I can't remember the exact thing I was doing when the explosion came. I think I was tasked with hitting the makiwara repeatedly and my effort was less than adequate. The makiwara is a length of wood planted into the ground. Around the top twine is wrapped tightly to create a striking surface to callous the knuckles. You would stand in a low stance focused on the task, make your hands into fists, and strike the post repeatedly using the first two knuckles. These would swell and scar up, sometimes growing to golf ball size protrusions that I am convinced lead to arthritis. If you hit it wrongly the wood would rebound back and send shockwaves coursing up your arm while snapping the wrist out at odd angles creating acute pain.

I had been slacking; the night before had been a long one and I felt rubbish. At that age I could drag myself around with a hangover and that's what I was doing. This morning though Sensei had had enough, and he very loudly berated me for my lack of effort. He made it very clear that I was wasting his time and disrespecting the art and the dojo by turning up this way. My eyes grew wide as I cowered under his wrath; it was the first time I had ever heard him swear and it was aimed at me. Suddenly he stopped; it was as if he had remembered where he was. He grabbed the base of his gi jacket and angrily jerked it down. He glared at me for a few seconds while he composed himself, then spun on his heels and walked to the other end of the dojo. Stunned I went back to striking the hard surface of the makiwara. Not another word was spoken that morning as I threw strike after strike while trying to surreptitiously look at the clock without invoking further anger. Eventually the time was up, and I slunk off to get changed.

The next day I was back at the dojo and feeling very sorry for myself. By this stage I had convinced myself that I didn't deserve the dressing down and the whole thing was very unfair. So, I took my thoughts to my other sensei who nodded sagely as I gave him my obviously biased version of events. It didn't seem fair. I stated that I worked so hard, much harder than the other students and still got shouted out. It wasn't fair! I carried on pressing my point exclaiming that I did more, trained more and worked harder yet here I was being berated like a naughty school kid.

'Would you prefer it never happened?' asked my sensei as he looked me dead in the eye. 'Of course,' I replied in the knee-jerk reaction of the terminally stupid. 'Don't you see the compliment you have been given?' he returned. His smile showed he was mildly amused by my confusion. 'I don't understand,' was all I could muster. I didn't understand. How could being yelled at ever be a good thing? Right now, it didn't feel good; in fact I had felt pretty lousy since it happened.

Sensei shifted in his seat and leaned forward conspiratorially. 'If Sensei had not thought you were worth his time, he would not have bothered shouting at you'. He continued, 'Because he got angry and let his emotions get the better of him momentarily, that shows that he cares enough about your progress to make the effort to get through. Shouting at you and giving you the chance to make it right is a compliment'. He ended his little speech with the words, 'Take it as such'. With that he smiled and got up from the chair, patting me on the shoulder as he left.

For a few minutes I sat there letting the words sink in. Never again would I misunderstand what it meant to be told off by Sensei. Without his belief in me I would have become just another ghost in the dojo.

11, HOW TO FAIL A GRADING WITHOUT TRYING.

I can't remember which leisure centre it was, as they all blend together in the mists of time, but I do remember this one was a few hours' drive from Bristol and had large steps leading up to the front. Thick iron railings ran up each side of the short, steady incline to the double sliding doors, with a separate ramp for wheelchair access. As always with these places the smell of the pool was one of the first things to reach your senses. We had gone through these doors on our way in, past the reception with its selection of impulse buys displayed along the back wall, and down the corridor lined with posters advertising the various classes they offered from the large sports hall that was to be our home for the weekend. This was a two-day event where instructors from as far afield as Japan had come to teach and oversee gradings. Everyone from white belt up could join in for the majority of the sessions so the hall was full of row upon row of crisp white gi's all snapping in unison.

The finale of the weekend was to be senior gradings but before that was a series of lessons covering all the different aspects of Karate. We did a physically intense session on kata which made my quads scream out and sweat drip from the end of my nose. Holding the stance low before moving to the next position on Sensei's command was a personal agony, but you didn't dare move or lift yourself slightly for momentary relief for fear of being singled out. You did not want to let yourself down in front of some of the most well-respected instructors in the world. Body resistance and stress positions, which in essence is what this was, created a whole-body workout that was incredibly hard to do with full commitment. The temptation to try to take it easy on yourself is great in these moments, but the instructors will know. They see all, and even in a room full of a hundred people the slightest lapse in effort is met with a glare of disapproval and a renewed sense of effort.

By this stage my feet were starting to bear the brunt of all the twisting and stepping movements. Incrementally the skin had been separating from the balls of my feet and the undersides of my big toes to leave large, open blisters that would pick up the grit and dirt from the hard wooden floor. Our dojo had mats down, so my feet had lost that rough, calloused armour that regular wooden floor training produces. I was lamenting that fact now as I stepped into position and snapped out my punch, twisting on the end. My gi now soaked with sweat had stopped making that sound a crisp, freshly washed gi does.

Instead it clung to me, saturated with the physical manifestation of my efforts. Every drop of sweat was a payment for knowledge, and every hidden wince of pain as my feet churned off another layer of protective skin was another moment where I was learning to marshal my mind to overcome my body.

Unlike a lot of training today, health and safety and our personal welfare appeared secondary as water breaks were a complete no. You were expected to finish the entire session without a drink, gulping down large quantities of liquids in the allocated breaks between sessions. It was not entirely uncommon to see students topple over in a faint like the unfortunate soldiers weighed down by their bearskins at the trooping of the colour. Training like this was a test of fortitude and self-control; could you withstand what was being asked or would you crumble under the pressure?

The grading itself was a test where you would be asked to perform a set series of movements. You would show your technique to the panel and if it was good enough you would pass. Or at least until that day that was what I naively thought.

It was a much-needed break in the training, and we had fifteen minutes to use the toilet, get a drink and wolf down a banana. A small percentage had another hunger to feed in those gaps and headed for the doors out into the sunshine. As it was a summer's day the heat in the hall had been stifling and the only concession given was that the fire doors had been propped open, creating the illusion of a cooling breeze. Psychologically we felt cooler; physically it made no difference to our sodden bodies. This was the door this brown belt headed to.

He was with two or three friends and they all put on flip flops and disappeared from view around the outside of the building. Here they hurriedly pulled out their cigarette brand of choice and lit up. I had seen the brown belt earlier and his form was good; he was working hard and from what I could see doing everything that was asked of him in the sessions. I knew that grading weekends like this meant you were being assessed the whole time and it appeared so did he, as his work rate was consistent. They stood in a small huddle where the occasional word of the conversation floated over as I stood in the doorway, gratefully sipping my bottled water.

Two of the Japanese instructors walked by me and as they came through the doorway, they were close enough to me that I had to take a little sidestep to let them pass. They noticed the brown belt and his entourage in their little circle; they watched him for a moment chatting away, oblivious to the decision that was being made and then wielded like Thor's hammer over his immediate future. The one turned to the other: 'He will fail, stupid habit,' he said as he pointed to the group. I avoided eye contact as they passed me, not knowing if they knew I had heard them or if they even cared.

I remained standing there for a few more minutes, leant against the frame of the door while I mulled over what I had just heard and what that could mean. Looking over at the brown belt I wondered if he knew his fate had already been decided and that the action of taking a quick smoke break had scuppered any chance of a black belt for him today. As they chatted, I knew he had no idea and as they turned and made their way back we briefly made eye contact as he went through the door. I smiled and gave a little nod. I didn't know the guy but now felt a certain camaraderie for him as I felt I was now part of his story and he (which is now true) part of mine. I momentarily toyed with the idea of telling him what I had heard but my better judgement overrode that impulse and I quietly returned to training with thoughts of this guy refusing to let go - which meant the remainder of the training was not focused and it showed.

The brown belt participated in the test and did what was asked. He went through his grading to the best of his ability with determination and technique. Already exhausted from the weekend's training, he dug deep into that part of us that lies dormant in everyone and forced his body to complete the test.

At the end he stood exhausted and spent to be told that he had failed. It appeared the instructors had let him continue to take the test knowing he was going to fail. And he would not be failing on his ability, but on the fact that he went for a sly fag and one of the sensei disapproved. Now it is not my place to judge this action or to give an opinion as to whether it was right or wrong, but this was the first time I had seen gradings treated so arbitrarily with no explanation as to why the person failed.

Now as I grade others to their black belt I sometimes wonder what happened to him. Did he return to finally achieve his goal or did he allow this failure to beat him? During the years I have seen people pass the black belt test but fail the black belt responsibilities. I have also seen students fail the test but come back better and stronger. In fact, I even know instructors who openly state that failing their black belt grading was the making of them.

As we move forward there is a perception that the coveted black belt is becoming nothing more than a weak shadow of its former self. I cannot speak for other clubs or organisations, but I can say this with certainty. To me the black belt should be held to the highest standard and the student who receives one accepts the responsibilities that come with it. It should not be so easy almost anyone can achieve it and whatever the world does around me doesn't matter, as anyone who earns the grade of black belt from me has spent years working hard to make it happen.

The belt is nothing more than a symbol of the journey. The knowledge and self-awareness should be the true prize.

12, THE BATTLE OF THE BIG TOE.

It sounds like a scene from early American history. A time when the brave red man held off the charging cavalry against appalling odds to protect his ancestral homeland. I picture the landscape of a John Ford western where the sky is never-ending, and the men are tough. Truth is I had broken my big toe and it was throbbing like a Belisha beacon at a school crossing. It's funny how your mind focuses on things and my mind was definitely fixated on the biggest digit on my left foot.

I had broken it the day before in free sparring. My badly timed sweep had connected with the shin of a guy who held black belts in multiple arts; think immovable object meets irresistible force. He stood six four at just shy of twenty stone. His leg muscles stood out against the cuffs of his gi bottoms and my foot had connected with his shin. Pain shot through me instantly as my toes collided with bone and my big toe was forced back under impact. I continued with the classes, but the pain was really kicking in.

This is where the hangover came to pass. Paracetamol was doing nothing and after shoving the best part of a pack down my gullet I needed another solution. Alcohol seemed to be my saviour at this point. Every drink I had led to less throbbing, until eventually the pain was replaced by a drunken haze that demanded food. I had no idea of time at this point, but my guess was it must have been at least two am. I had to be up in less than four hours. We had shared a chalet to cut costs and in my inebriated state I conceded any beds for the couch. There I fell, sandwich in hand, blissfully pain free but about to suffer the consequences of my pain management choices very soon.

'Get up!' was shouted at me. I gingerly opened one eye to find the chalet a hive of activity. Bodies rushed backwards and forwards as my eyes tried to adjust and the room slowly swam into focus. I swung my legs off the sofa and sat up; as I did so last night's half-eaten ham and cheese baguette slid from my cheek to land in my lap. I looked down at the remains of the roll with the shape of my teeth running down its crushed edge, trying to remember exactly how I got here. My musings were shattered as my gi hit me in the side of the head. I was snapped out of my reverie to the realisation that in fifteen minutes I would have to run six miles in the sand in bare feet with a broken big toe.

I sobered up pretty quick.

The shower was a mixture of haste, meaning I had to rush not to be late, and gingerly exploring every weight shift on my foot as my toe had woken up with me. It's very hard to put on gi pants hungover, half-awake and in a hurry; it's even harder if this challenge is like a 3D version of the game *Operation*. One wrong move forced my foot to hit the material and my nose didn't light up, but the buzzer certainly went off in my head and expletives would pour from my mouth like a Deep South preacher speaking in tongues.

I flip-flopped my way through the chalets to the beach and this morning's rendezvous point. Tying my belt as I went and walking like one of those urban gangsta kids with the fake limp, I tried to readjust the shoulder strap on my kit bag so that it hurt less. I got there with minutes to spare, so while the others limbered up and stretched I threw a couple of paracetamols down my neck and frantically taped my toes together, wrapping them tightly so they were bound side by side to offer less freedom of movement. This would present its own problems later when trying to put the flip flops back on, but that was the least of my worries.

The beach that morning was deserted apart from a couple walking their dog in the distance, and it slowly curved off into the horizon to meet the jagged outcrops of rocks that swept out to meet the sea. The morning sun reflected off the wet sand as the surf rolled in and out, tumbling bunches of seaweed and debris on its waves to deposit them along the shoreline as the shrill high-pitched squawks of the sea birds carried in the wind. The sun was not yet fully risen, and the stretch of beach looked postcard perfect in its morning glow.

There were around twenty of us on the run. Not all were grading; some were there because they enjoyed running in the morning. I have already mentioned my distaste for such things; over the years it is something I have done many times whether it was training for a fight or during a grading as in now, and it never gets enjoyable. I am aware some people drift off into a Zen-like state and run for hours in their happy place, but that is not me. I am not built for running and never enjoy it, but I am stubborn as a mule, and when I set myself to a physical task doggedness and determination rather than talent are what see me through.

Once during my secondary school education, I showed this mindset to prove a point. I have already mentioned the teacher involved who was a rugger bugger bullying type. He had those really large upper legs that he proudly displayed in his shorts, and a protruding eyebrow ridge to physically prove he was nearer to Neanderthal man than me. He appeared to base his entire judgement of a person's character on their ability in sports. Nerds and bookworms look out, as this bully would actively try to humiliate you to show off his physical prowess.

To him I was a waste of his time. I had already blotted my copybook by not wanting to participate in team sports. None of the activities on offer at the school appealed to me, but I did like chess, and I was pretty good. I could also draw pretty well and ask intelligent questions. I had an urge to prick pomposity even then, and would rile him to fits of indignation with my total lack of enthusiasm for games and impertinent questioning as to the pointlessness of the activity. I played rugby for five minutes and quickly realised cold Sunday mornings in the drizzle and mud while wearing shorts was not my thing. Football to me was the most pointless waste of my life ever, so that really only left track and running.

At that age I had asthma and it would come and go. As the years went on it finally disappeared altogether in my teens, which I am very grateful for. But for now, I was still victim to occasional attacks. For me it was a perfect excuse to get out of the mundane PE lessons, so I would often use this to manipulate my exclusion from the session. This was another reason for the teacher to dislike me as he knew I was swinging the lead, and I knew that he knew, but was powerless to stop me.

This particular morning it was time for a cross country run. We were supposed to run from the school through the woods to an abandoned manor house and back again. The run was reasonably flat with a slight incline, but the weather was that cold, grey drizzle and the paths were muddy. Today I was going to prove a point. Normally I did not participate in these, or if I did, I would dawdle along at the back, sacrificing my break so as not to break a sweat. But today the four-and-a-half-mile track would be used for a different purpose.

I can't remember why exactly, but I decided to run it properly. In the pack were two county level runners and a number of members from the different sports teams the school would compete in. As the run progressed, I easily kept pace with the front runners and began to edge out and away from the main pack. Finding my breathing rhythm, I kept focused on the edge of my field of vision, concentrating on that finishing line, one foot after the other clearing ground to land and propel me even faster forward towards that goal. As a tall gangly kid back then my stride was long, and my determined gait ate through the miles.

I came second. Mr Rugger Bugger looked perplexed as I had just outrun his favourites. He was even more perplexed when the next time I went right back to mooching along with the other so-called losers. No amount of coercion, threats or pleading would get me to do that again. I had proved the point that I could, and that was enough for me.

Fast forward again to my black belt grading, and the run that I was now on became an exercise in control. As my bare feet hit the wet sand my toes would have to dig in for grip to claim enough purchase to carry the momentum forward. My calves were swollen with blood and were working at maximum to counteract the spongy, damp surface. Each time my foot landed a fresh wave of pain would shoot through me, and each time I gripped the sand, needles would stab me all up my leg. My lower back was also really hurting as I had been running off-balance to try to take some of the edge off. It hadn't worked and had only served to make my predicament worse. The sun was rising, and the salty breeze offered the light caress of its soothing coolness. Occasionally the spray from the surf would reach high enough to spatter my chest and head to mingle with the sweat that was running freely from me.

Locked into my own private world of physical feelings I almost lost a sense of reality. The people around me disappeared as I focused inward. The pain was relentless, and each fresh wave jarred me, but they were consistent. As I knew they would come I could prepare myself mentally; I focused on each one as the steady thud of my feet grew monotonous and I timed them. The only things in my consciousness in that moment were the sound of the surf breaking on the shoreline and my feet landing on the moist sand. Nothing else was real or existed to me. Maybe this was the nirvana real runners feel? Could this be the Zen state that people claim running gives them? Maybe I needed the pain to focus myself fully on the task and that was my gateway to clarity? I don't know if any of that was the case, but eventually I finished the run and the world swam back into view.

This was not the end of my day, but the start, and hard, wooden sports hall floors awaited me. Hour after hour of pair work, technique and forms still stood between me and my goal. No quarter would be given, and I would be expected to do exactly the same as everyone else.

I passed. It was a moment I will remember, as this was my reward for the years of hard work and sacrifice I had put in. No one but me knew the personal sacrifices I had endured, and the cost for those around me in my pursuit of this goal. Obviously, I was not alone, and everyone has their own individual tale to tell, but it felt important to me to recognise those struggles and know I had overcome them. But the prize was not the belt. The real prize was mastery of myself that day. Just for a fleeting moment I became the master of my own destiny. For that day I was not the debris swept this way and that by the tides of circumstance. For that day I was the frigate cutting through the waves, sleek and single-minded in the pursuit of my goal. The real reward was seeing that in myself and becoming it, if only for a day. Knowing that surely meant it would be easier to do it again. I learned that there is steel in us all and we can rise to the occasion, and on this day I had.

Many years later, I had been notified of the dates for my fourth dan grading. It was going to be held in Doncaster at Andy Crittenden's club. I have had the privilege to visit this fantastic club many times and the welcome is always warm. Under the knowledgeable scrutiny of Master Dave Turton, I would be asked to partake in the weekend and also teach. I think to say I was nervous was an understatement as among the people sharing their expertise on this weekend were some absolute legends. Among them were high grades, UFC referees, undefeated fighters, and personal friends. This was a big pond I was swimming in, and these guys were at the top of the game.

All the instructors teaching that weekend were top quality and I would be expected to deliver my teaching segment to this standard. The legend that is Trevor Roberts gave an absolute masterclass. Known as the Bolton Iron Man, he is the most humble and friendly person you could ever wish to meet. His humour is great which he proved as we sat captivated as he told us the story of the only time her ever lost a fight. I won't spoil it by revealing what happened, but if you ever get a chance, ask him to tell it to you. Neil Hall who has reffed for the UFC took a turn. A powerhouse of a man with vast amounts of knowledge behind him, he led us through a great technical session. Paul Oxtoby took to the mats to help us all to improve our kicks. Whenever someone remarks on the inadequacies of TKD and claims it doesn't work I point them towards Paul. The man could fell a bull elephant with those kicks. I have witnessed the power in his kicks first-hand and can assure the readers that they are not the tippy tappy kind. Master Dave did a session and as always made the painful even more so. The self-deprecating humour and ready smile hide a vault of martial knowledge that has taken over fifty years to accumulate. He uses the phrase: *feeling is believing*, and I have never met anyone before or since who could create such pain with such economy of movement.

I had heard the name Dave Turton many times over the years from a lot of people I respected and so wanted to seek him out. I was not disappointed. The first time I met Dave was at the very gym where I was going to do my grading. I had arranged to drive halfway across the country to meet and learn from the man himself. It was instantly obvious that here was someone who was the real deal. Capable and knowledgeable, but without that air of self-importance that often follows lesser instructors around like the unpleasant odour that lingers in the air from a fart, he did not demand titles and honorific names. Yet his demeanour meant that you gave them freely as those accolades were earned and well deserved.

My turn came and I was greeted with a room full of expectant faces. I have noticed that a lot of martial arts people struggle to use focus pads correctly. Maybe they misunderstand the point of these tools, or maybe they have just never been shown properly. If you are interested in learning how to use these properly yourself, I would steer you towards Mittmaster Matt, who is very knowledgeable on this topic. Back to my own humble teachings on the subject and I wanted to sort out the problem of Mickey Mouse ears. I hope Disney doesn't sue.

Picture the cartoon character in your mind and visualise those big round ears like dinner plates sticking out the side of his head. This is how a lot of people hold pads; with the pads high and wide they look like Mickey Mouse. Now, as no one aside from the Elephant Man has a three-foot head, having them that far apart actually instils bad technique into the practitioner. All they are learning is how not to punch properly. Personal trainers are equally as inept at this for the most part. So, my job for today was to teach some basic focus pad drills using proper form. We had fun with it and the group seemed to get something from it, with the comments positive when we talked afterwards.

My assessment done, we continued with the weekend culminating in the presentation of my fourth dan certificate. I had spent the weekend camped out in the yard of the gym in my van, and so with two full days of training under my belt coupled with the joys of sleeping on a camp bed in the back of my transit I was tired, sore and stiff. But it was worth every moment as I stood there receiving my certificate from Master Dave as the late afternoon sun beamed in through the windows. The photos of that presentation look like we are in some sort of tractor beam from a sci-fi movie but remain a proud moment for me. To achieve that in front of so many people I admired meant a lot, and knowing that being around such inspirational people could only make my martial arts better, I realised that this was another step on the path.

Once more I had outstretched my hand and reached up to the people above on the journey. They in turn had reached back to generously give their knowledge to help me take the next steps. Once again it was obvious that for us to grow, we need each other, and for us to succeed we must be instrumental in helping others to find success.

From past, to present, to future.

We had travelled down to Exeter to participate in a Bill 'Superfoot' Wallace seminar. The American kickboxing legend is an amazing man and someone whom I recommend everyone should try to meet. He was in his seventies I believe by now and walked into the sports hall with the individual walk he has, wearing baggy, blue gi pants and a greying sweatshirt. He led the warm-up and dropped into the full box splits while grinning at us and chattering away non-stop as he does. 'I recommend the cheeseburger diet,' he was saying. 'Oils the joints with all that fat'. The humour did not disguise either his knowledge or ability as he led us through the session. I held a bag for a demonstration of his legendary side kick. I was glad of three things in that moment. One: I had a kick shield between me and him. Two: he was in his seventies, as in his prime he would certainly have launched me across the room. Three: he didn't mean it. The fire of a fighter that lies behind his eyes is only slightly veiled by the humour in his teaching style and you just know that that switch still exists.

I had some students with me on this trip, a father and son who had been training with me for a number of years. Dad was a first dan black belt under me and his son Harvey who was ten at the time had just passed his purple belt with us. I had arranged for Superfoot to present Harvey with his new belt and it was a wonderful thing to witness. Harvey's eyes showed confusion when Superfoot called him forward, but the confusion gave way to a Cheshire Cat smile when he realised what was happening. Superfoot asked him to remove his current belt and with great humility tied the new purple belt around Harvey's waist. All the time he was doing this he was offering words of encouragement to him. His dad was literally bursting with pride at this point as he had followed Superfoot for years and knew what this meant.

We watched this magical moment, and to see someone so far up the mountain take the time to reach so far back is a testament to the man. Wherever Harvey goes and whatever his life turns out to be he will never forget the time when Bill 'Superfoot' Wallace presented him with his belt. That will be etched into his memory and very soul, and one day in years to come, if the world is allowed to turn full circle, he will reach down to help a young coloured belt and give them that treasured moment.

I think it is a responsibility for us all to pass on the knowledge that was passed to us. We do not own it, even though we worked so hard to cultivate it. We are part of a wider whole, an ecosystem that needs new growth to survive and flourish. Our task is to share that knowledge and help the next generation to discover what an amazing gift the martial arts can be. If we make that part of our personal promise to the world then that can only enhance our own practice.

PART 3.
REACHING OUT.

Real knowledge is to know the
extent of one's ignorance.

Confucius.

13, THE END OF AN ERA.

There were lots of little factors involved in my choice, but it was two main turning points for me that cemented my decision to move away from the traditional and sport side of the martial arts. Never rejecting it, but more a shift of focus in both my personal training and goals.

The first turning point was a physical injury.

I was practising Karate and had been competing to the point where I had been offered the opportunity to go to fight in Europe with the team. I remember going to get my passport in eager anticipation of getting on that coach and representing. But it was not to be this time.

I had been in a competition a few weeks earlier; as always the hall was alive with nervous chatter. The hall had been hired from a sports centre; the space was large, and voices echoed in the space. Basketball nets were folded up to the closed position in the roof and the partition nets were tied back against the wall to allow the maximum use of the hall. There were four fighting areas set up: square matted areas with two short lengths of tape in the middle to signify where the fighters should stand. Seats were set up around the square for the points judges, and the fighters were expected to kneel in rows along the edge of the matted areas when their group was called. Rows of seats ran the length of the hall up the one side for the spectators to sit and in the top corner was a small designated warm-up area for the participants to stretch and get ready.

As always, the competitors would be wearing their club tops over their gi's and would be looking around to spot likely opponents. Most would have large kit bags with the side pockets stuffed with cereal bars and bananas. The families claimed their spots in the viewing areas and slowly the hall began to fill.

On the wall was posted an itinerary; the running order always put the kids first, but we still had to be there for registration by ten am. The overseeing body had also implemented the rule that all medallists had to wait until the end for the presentation and must remain in their gi throughout. This made for a long day with maybe three fights if you took an average. I would tend to go in for the individual, team and kata sections as this would give me the most opportunity to compete. This strategy didn't always work in my favour as often I would be racing from mat to mat, not warmed up, mentally unprepared or both. It was also expected that we would support our fellow club members and be there to cheer them on in their fights as well. The days were always a strange mix of time-distorting waiting mixed with bursts of frenetic activity.

I had been called. With my group I lined up alongside the mat. As one we all bowed to the opposing row facing us. We knelt unmoving in our lines as the fighters were called. This was an agonising time as not only were the nerves kicking in, but the posture of kneeling meant that pretty soon your legs went numb and the circulation got hampered. Pins and needles followed by cramps as the muscles seized up meant that you prayed to get out there as soon as you could.

Finally, my turn arrived and as I bowed and walked onto the mat, I assessed my opposite number while we took our places at the tape. We were asked to bow to the referee and then to each other. We took fighting stance and waited for the command to be given. Karate points fighting is a mix of skill, speed, timing, and accuracy. No full contact blows are allowed but almost always the fighting got fierce and more than once competitors including myself were penalised for excessive contact. The aim was to score a clean blow with foot or fist. A *wazari* was a half point and meant you had scored a clean shot. An *ippon* score was worth a full point and signified what would have been a killing blow. Not as in deadly, but in the sense that if thrown with intent and power that strike would have ended the match.

'Hajime'. The Japanese word was barked loudly as the ref dropping his arm between us galvanised me into action and I instantly darted forward, determined to get the first point and the upper hand. The fight was fast and both of us had scored some good shots when calamity happened. I badly broke my little finger; not just broke it but shattered the bone.

The gloves we wore offered little protection and were thinly cushioned padding that covered our knuckles. Our fingers fed through elasticated hoops that held the gloves in place. Mine were white and had a well-known brand name emblazoned across the top.

I had grabbed my opponent and performed a sweep, bunching his gi in my hand and twisting my fist as I reaped his legs from underneath him. His legs flew out to waist height as his torso jack-knifed towards the floor. My hand was stuck, wrapped in the collar of his gi, and the full weight of his body went through my little finger as he crashed to the floor with me following him.

I had broken fingers and toes before and although painful, I thought would it heal given time. I had spent long enough in accident and emergency rooms surrounded by the drunks and germs of a city centre casualty unit, only to be told there was nothing they could do, to want to do that again. At that time, I was working as a painter and decorator, and spent the week climbing ladders and crawling on my knees painting skirting boards, as my hand swelled and got blacker and blacker.

The pain was a constant throb that never left; any accidental pressure to it resulted in expletives and a very ungraceful dance that lasted about a minute. The swelling had got to the point where my hand looked like someone had blown up a Marigold glove and the bruising which had gone from deep purples to an almost black colour had spread up my wrist. It was time to admit defeat and go to the hospital.

X-rays were taken and much was made of the fact I had been working the whole time. They didn't understand the concept that as a self-employed person with no financial back-up from anyone the motivation was simple. You don't work, you don't eat. As employed, professional, salaried staff they found the idea of this difficult to grasp. As we looked at the results, the female doctor using a biro pointed to the wreck that used to be my finger and explained to me the extent of the damage and what could be done.

The finger was strapped to its neighbour, my arm was slung to my chest and the rehabilitation process began. For a year my hand was wrapped and my fingers taped. I managed to go back to training after some time and with the help of my instructors I tried to work around the injury as best as I could.

The competition rules at the time stated a competitor could not start a competition with taped-up fingers. This was my first fight back after the injury and it had been a long difficult road. The fight started, I threw a punch and my worst fears came to fruition. My hand exploded in pain as my damaged finger disintegrated on impact.

A whole year had been wasted as I was right back to square one. Work had suffered, training had suffered, and my mental well-being was in the balance as sometimes a sense of depression sunk over me in a fog. I remember one day going to the specialty unit where we were seriously considering amputating it for a short while. Whilst I was sat in the waiting room a family came in: Mum, Dad and two pretty young girls around seven or eight. Both had pigtails but one of the girls had both hands fully encased in this metal scaffolding. Pins protruded through her skin and connected to the framework that ran around both hands. I could not help but overhear as the one sister was telling the other not to worry as she would help her to open her presents at Christmas. She had been in a car accident and both hands had been crushed. Everything she needed was having to be done by other people. She was helpless, but the smile on her face and the easy laughter the sisters shared showed that she wasn't going to be beaten by it. In that moment I felt tremendous guilt. I had been wallowing in self-pity and allowed myself to believe in the dark voices whispering in my ear. It took a young child to make me see what I was doing to myself.

Once again, the process of healing began. I now have pins holding my finger together. I have lost about two centimetres in length where it was compacted and because I was taped up for so long my two fingers on that hand have now moulded to the shape of one another and fit flush together. My hands are damaged and scarred with many broken bones, scars and callouses and they tell the stories of those times. From the makiwara training to the doorwork and competitions, my hands bore the brunt over the years and even now I still can't make a proper fist with one hand.

Fight, flight, or freeze.

The second incident that led to my decision to look towards other ways of doing things happened on a sunny Sunday morning and caught me unawares. It was my own lack of knowledge that had brought me here, and again my lack of knowledge that allowed the situation to unfold the way that it did.

Now I am not going to name the person in this story as he doesn't deserve the oxygen of publicity. He had been to prison many times before for violent offences including armed robbery and was back inside a few weeks after this incident for racially motivated GBH on a local shop owner. The worst part of this whole sorry tale for me was that in my own arena, with my rules, I would have eaten him alive without breaking a sweat. Knowing this made the lesson even more of a bitter pill to swallow. Just in case this gets back to the person in question: if you disagree with any of this feel free to get in touch.

I had heard through the local grapevine that he wanted to see me. As it was a Sunday morning and the sun was shining, I didn't want to be stuck in the house so thought this would be a perfect opportunity to see what he wanted. He was known for violence and had a long history of such. Most people avoided him while he and his hard-drinking mates would physically force their arrested development on the punters in the local bars.

That should have been enough to make me wary, but I had no reason to think he wished me bad intent at that point. I was wrapped up in my own perceived abilities to handle things and honestly thought this was nothing more than a social chat regards some mutual acquaintances.

As his house was a ten-minute drive from mine, I jumped in the car; back then I had a newish red Ford estate. I had left the dog at the house and backed off the driveway. The sun was shining so I pushed the button to make the window slide down and cranked up the stereo. Neil Diamond was banging out his greatest hits and I was singing along enthusiastically. The short journey was soon over, and I turned the corner into his street where his rented council house sat at the end of a row of identical houses. He was already outside and before I had even finished pulling up, he launched a bomb of a right hand through the open window into the side of my face. My head shot back as my mind desperately tried to catch up with events. I had pulled up tight to the car in front, and still had my seat belt trapping me in. His bodyweight was against the door as he rained down a flurry of punches filled with bad intent. Instinct or maybe limited training kicked in and I shifted in my seat and covered up. That first sucker punch was the only one to land; the rest bounced harmlessly off arms and shoulders. However, the damage had been done; my eye instantly began to swell. The punch had been executed well and had caught me completely off guard.

I wriggled and pushed and forced him to back off at which point he ran towards his house, reached around his front door and pulled out a baseball bat. At that moment I will be honest and say my mind was easily five steps behind at this point, and I was struggling to register what was happening. He prowled along the fence line threatening me with the bat. It was then that I chose to drive away. I had been ambushed and had lost the battle. I went back two weeks later and stood knocking on his front door alone and ready for war. The greeting I received that time was very different, and the matter was sorted there and then. No police were involved as that is not how things like that are solved. It was only a few short weeks after that he was banged up again for more stupid violence.

The immediate aftermath is what is interesting in this story. I had frozen. In the moment, adrenaline has dumped itself on me; my training to that point had not geared me towards such an attack and truth is, I was mentally and physically unprepared. The problem was I held black belts and titles, had won trophies and competitions, and worked the doors as a bouncer. In my mind I was nigh on invincible. Truth is my own vanity and false perception of my abilities had left me weak and vulnerable.

At first, like most people who go through this, I lied to myself. I made excuses and tried to soothe my battered ego with lies made up to comfort me. Every time I looked in the mirror and saw my swollen, purple eye I made an excuse about what happened. I told myself that I had not allowed myself to batter him as I would lose my license to work in security. I told myself that I didn't want the criminal charges and court case. I even told myself that I let him off as I was scared that with my training, I would really hurt him. You know, all the usual lies we tell ourselves. After a few days of this, it was time to own up to the truth. I just wasn't trained for anything other than the dojo or the ring. So far, I had gotten away with it, and my time on the doors up till now had helped me to believe my own hype. This needed to change.

14, WHAT'S IN A NAME?

The traditional Karate had progressed to some other things, and while still training in those methods I was also exploring other ways. One of my instructors at the time was not just a very well-respected karateka but also a kickboxer and bouncer. Standing at around five ten and around thirteen stone he was not a big man but had a presence that was much larger. He had a massive amount of knowledge, was a huge influence on my training, and opened my mind to the possibilities out there.

Every Saturday morning at ten am I would have a private lesson with him. We would work through kata and technique as I tried to improve. These sessions were invaluable to me and apart from the odd time where I found myself hitting myself with a stick for conditioning, I learned a great deal over that period. I was also lucky enough to be involved in some more freestyle type training with him as he had drawn students to him from different backgrounds. In this small group was a South African doorman. He rarely smiled and was a big powerful guy that practised kickboxing. A father and son, the father was a large solid man with dan grades in Judo. He was so solid I broke two of my toes on his shin once. But these guys paled in comparison to the vision that lay before me that day.

I had walked through those big red doors to be met by Sensei's smiling face. Something was up, I could tell. At the time the cramped changing area was downstairs with a row of small reinforced glass windows that looked out to the training area. I took off my jacket and glanced through the window. The glance became a stare as in my vision stood a man mountain of truly epic proportions. Stretching on the mats in a pair of vale tudo shorts was a guy; he stood six four and must have easily been twenty stone. His legs were like tree trunks and his hugely muscular frame rippled as he moved. His name was James 'The Colossus' Thompson and he was an MMA fighter who had come to do some training with Sensei to work on his striking in preparation for an upcoming fight.

We trained as a small group for a while with me at six two being the smallest in the sessions, and they were tough. But that being said, I was now in the best physical shape of my life and felt sharp and strong.

It was here where we would get involved and share ideas. Kickboxing took on a more important role for me as I was getting more and more frustrated with points fighting. I had recently been wrongfully penalised for repeatedly kicking the leg when I had actually been sweeping. Being a leftie, it was a go-to technique of mine as I was often placed with my lead leg just to the outside of theirs. Combine that with the now almost constant warnings for excessive contact and I was losing interest in that competition format rapidly. Things like boxers' hooks and Thai low kicks became things I needed to master, and I could not get those from the Karate I had been practising.

The South African kickboxer and I would regularly travel together to train. Aside from the other training we were both doing we would get in the car and drive the hour and fifteen-minute journey to the gym in Bridgewater where we would join in with the kickboxing classes once a week. These were different to the structured Karate classes of old and everyone spoke in English. Sweat would run freely from us as we hit pads and bags for round after round. Cardio was a must, so a lot of time was given to fitness, which was needed to push through the rounds of sparring.

I found a lot of the full contact training to be really enjoyable. The results were not some promised will-o'-the-wisp future expertise, but real and in the now. The pads would talk to you and tell you if you were improving. The sound of a focus mitt being hit right is different to the sound if it is not. The power of the shot would feel good as the impact ran up your arm. The endless rounds of bagwork were gratifying as we would skip around throwing combinations and power shots.

The improvement was rapid and here was something I enjoyed as it combined the skill and beauty of the Karate with the added skills of boxing, Thai and other striking styles all put together in a full contact setting. Many years earlier I had clipped one of my instructors with a hooking style punch during sparring that had rocked him. He had told me then that I had knockout power, and now I was getting to develop it.

Fight night came and I was sat at a ringside table as James 'The Colossus' Thompson did his walk on. The MC had announced him as the strobe lights ran a pattern over the heads of the cheering crowd. He stepped through the fog of dry ice and made his way down the gangway as his signature tune played. As he walked towards the ring his eyes were piercing; he was focused on the job in hand. Tonight, he would fight the living legend that is Dan 'The Beast' Severn. Dan had been around for years at the elite level and was one of the best, first appearing on UFC 2. He was a wrestler who had just missed out on the Olympics but had gone on to fight the very best over decades. In later interviews he admitted to underestimating James, even suggesting that he assumed him to be nothing more than a muscle-bound gym bunny.

In the corner for the fight were Arthur Meek and Kevin O'Hagan, two very well-respected local instructors. James's corner had the best knowledge the South West had to offer going into that fight, but that didn't stop the nerves. James stood in his corner pacing from one foot to the other while he rolled his head from side to side in an effort not to tense up. James has admitted to being so nervous before fights that he would often throw up, but that moment would pass as he made his way to the cage.

James won the fight and the whole place erupted as the local boy had done it. I remember both Arthur Meek and Kevin O'Hagan hugging the sweat-drenched Colossus in a little victory celebration. If my memory serves me, I'm pretty sure that Kevin at one point jumped up and planted a smacker on the side of James's head. Dan Severn walked right past me on his exit and you could see the loss weighed heavily on him. That was the last event that promotion put on and it was now time for everyone to move on. James went on to fight some of the biggest names in some of the biggest promotions in MMA history, and represented across the world.

15, WRESTLING, BUT NOT THE SATURDAY AFTERNOON KIND.

Having had a taste of things outside Karate I wanted to explore the world of martial arts and see what else was out there. This was around twenty-five years ago now and I still had some gangliness to my frame, but I had at least cut my hair by then.

Another shop window poster had brought me to this part of town which was in a working-class residential area. Along this side of the main street was a row of shops and through a door and up some stairs led to the training area above. It looked like abandoned offices or similar with those large metal-framed windows that swung open in the middle. They were filthy from the constant grime that was spat out from the exhausts of the buses that passed every fifteen minutes or so.

The flyer hadn't promised much but offered Olympic-style wrestling. At that point I knew nothing of the style other than I kept getting my arse dragged to the floor in the mixed sparring we had been doing and wanted that to stop.

I was greeted by a shortish guy who was the instructor. In the room were maybe ten or twelve others. As they prepared, I was instantly struck by the fact that all of them were heavily muscled. Not in a bodybuilding way where they were disproportionate to their size, but in a more athletic way that emphasised movement. It was to be proven true when we got to practising as these guys were incredibly strong and moved like lightning.

First, we had to lay out the mats, and then run a huge sheet of tight-fitting shiny tarp over them all. Then began the warm-up. Within minutes my muscles were screaming with the unfamiliar movements. We drilled and drilled these in a set of exercises that felt like they were designed to kill you. Finally, we stopped for a water break and to my horror the rest of the group were chatting and smiling to each other. I on the other hand was gasping for air like a landed fish. I was so far behind the curve that it was embarrassing.

When we got to the techniques, I was paired with this fifteen-year-old lad who was about my height and muscular. He had one of those half taches. It wasn't quite ready yet, but he was proud to be becoming a man and wasn't going to shave it off. Any feelings of age-related superiority soon left me as he moved through the techniques with smooth efficiency. My muscles burned and my grip strength had faded to nothing from the warm-up alone as he coached me step-by-step through the movements.

I was still training a number of times a week in Karate and now doing two nights a week of this. Something had to give and after a few months we had reached a point where decisions needed to be made. The wrestling coach had been pushing me to compete. There was a competition coming up and a number from this club were taking part. I had avoided the last one but was running out of excuses this time. My main focus was still on my Karate training so when I was pushed to compete and up my training with this, the decision to leave the club was an easy one. They were a sport, and as such competition was a requirement for the students. As it was explained to me at the time: *The man who chases two buses catches neither*, and I had my own goals in mind.

It was a shame to leave as the coach was very good and the fellow students were a great bunch. My strength, movement and balance had all improved massively, and I had been introduced to a new level of pain that only grapplers understand. My wrestling stuttered there for a few years, but I have always stepped in and out of grappling. Never becoming really good, or even a little bit good as the learning curve is so steep now, and the level of knowledge available is so amazing it would be impossible to keep up without dedicating years of my life to its pursuit.

A few years later I was teaching at a gym in Bristol and they had a BJJ programme under one of the UK's best instructors. A few of the guys were coming up through the ranks and would often have open mat sessions. I had been working the doors for a while and occasionally I found myself on the floor, sometimes by choice, other times by circumstance. So, it seemed like a good idea to get back into some live rolling.

Turns out it was not a good idea. I had managed to get myself on the text list with these guys and so when an impromptu session was about to happen the texts would go around to the small group. Everyone would be smiling and joking, and the mood was always upbeat, but that did nothing to ease the pain of those hours. The timer would be set; a loud metallic bell sound would come from the big red box. We would face each other on our knees and then slap hands and bump knuckles. Next would begin the slow countdown to my almost inevitable tap. The guys were actively learning the system of BJJ; I was just rolling and picking up odd tips here and there to put in my own game. They would pull guard or manipulate my balance to claim a better position, incrementally closing me down as they cut me off. Eventually the choke would sink in or the joint would be hyperextended, and I would tap repeatedly with my hand to affect my release. Every three minutes the buzzer would go off and we would turn to face a new opponent and do it all again. As the session wore on my strength faded and my ability to fight back grew less so I tapped more.

These sessions were a great experience for me as they showed me that we all have our particular fields of expertise and my ego had to take a rain check. I once saw a very high level BJJ instructor hitting the pads. His footwork and delivery were that of a beginner. The punches had no power and his positioning made hitting him in the face like taking candy from a baby. And that's how it felt with me: candy from a baby. It was a great way to learn fast. Every time I rolled, I learned something and every time I was tapped, I learned something else. They do say the first year of BJJ is about surviving and learning to defend and I believe them. I have revisited various forms of grappling over the years, but she is nothing more than a mistress; my one true love will always be punching someone in the face.

16. KRAV IS LIKE A BOX OF CHOCOLATES. YOU NEVER KNOW WHAT YOU'RE GONNA GET. (SAID IN THE VOICE OF FORREST GUMP).

My path had led me firmly to the door of Krav Maga and KAPAP (a Hebrew acronym for Krav Panim el Panim). Here I found the level of knowledge and standard to range from the exceptionally good to the absurdly awful. I found very quiet, knowledgeable guys with many, many years of learning behind them, but I also found guys who made the famous Walter Mitty look grounded. And the unfortunate thing is that this situation is still the same. There is a huge discrepancy within the Krav Maga world and knowing which is which can be a hard task, hampered further by the constant online bad-mouthing of the various groups.

But amongst all of this, at its core lies a system born of necessity. The direct techniques driven by aggression and economy of the movements made this something I wanted to learn. The Krav Maga of years ago is a distant cousin to the bloated marketing behemoth you see today. The almost cult-like behaviour of some of the groups we now see did not exist like that originally and we now have belts and ranking systems, Krav for kids and several different organisations all claiming superiority. Then it was the rawness of the system that was its strength, and I wanted to find out more.

The people were born into a war zone and grew up among the soldiers and bombs. All politics aside the thing that strikes me most is that growing up under the constant threat of violence and death must be a hard life. Fearing for the safety of your family every second of every day must do something to the human psyche. Hard lives breed hard men. Some of the most intimidating people I have ever met have come from this background. Not musclebound or freakishly large, but dead eyes and a perception of steel that is felt rather than seen. These guys radiated the fact that you would have to kill them to stop them, and I believed that gut instinct.

I had signed up for a basic instructor course. At one point in my training I would sign up for a few of these. There were two main reasons for this. One is that this is how a lot of the Krav/KAPAP organisations format their training and two, I actually enjoyed this immersive style of doing things. The set-up was like a week-long seminar where you lived and breathed the process. Nine to ten hours' training every day till your body was so sore it hurt to move, followed by an evening meal with your fellow trainees. You ate, slept and shit nothing but martial arts for that week. You also got to meet some great people.

The course was being held up north and the drive up had been awful. We had left at around three am and the cold winter was biting. The plan was to drive through the rest of the night to save another evening's hotel bill. The wind howled at gale force levels and the rain came down in sheets. For the entire journey I peered through the windscreen as the wipers pushed away the downpour creating a momentary clear view. Vision was ten feet in front of the car at best as the headlights met the forces of Mother Nature and dulled into insignificance. The journey was over five hours and every mile demanded my full concentration.

We had made it and I was now stood in a room with maybe thirty others. On this course we were to have the best level instruction this organisation had to offer. Leading the training was going to be the head of the group, the lead man and founder. With him were two of his best instructors. All three of these men oozed confidence as they looked around the room. It seemed they were looking into our very souls as one by one they would lock their gaze with a student.

One of the instructors in particular stood out. Olive skinned with dark piercing eyes that looked out over a slightly hawkish nose. His blocky head sat upon a stocky powerful frame. Maybe a little under six foot and in his late forties, the raw power of the man emanated from him. He had done the full term in the elite forces of his country and had run small teams equivalent to our SAS into situations I could only imagine. His eyes appeared lifeless as he glared at me. Now was not the time to look away, so I met his gaze which was uncomfortable to hold. By this time, I had been training in various things for a number of years and didn't consider myself a novice, I stood six two at seventeen stone and had been a bouncer for a number of years. But that stare seemed to reach inside me and grab my insecurities, dragging them to the surface where they lay exposed and vulnerable. I had literally been examined and measured in that few seconds, or at least that is what it felt like.

Once the introductions were over the training started in earnest. The first day is always the worst. I have heard it described as the dickhead test. Basically, it is hour after hour of serious physical torture designed to push people to the edge of what they are capable of. Remember the history of the people running the show so you can get a feel of it. Endless drills that led to muscle fatigue and exhaustion. Group exercises that were designed to fail. All the while the instructors would be yelling and beasting us when we didn't give them the effort they thought we should. Almost always you lost some students in the breaks. They would just quietly sneak off, usually not saying a word. They just got in their car and drove back to wherever it was they came from. Often people sign up thinking it's an easy route, little realising the physical requirements needed just to get through that first day. It felt like a mini selection process which is exactly what it was. Weed out the weak and lose the ones who would slow down the group. By the end of the day we had lost a few, but those who remained were already starting to bond. We had faced the adversity together and now had common experiences to connect us. We started the day as strangers, but by the end of the week would form friendships that have lasted years.

Over the course of the week we learned a lot of things. The training had a military bent and some of it I found a little difficult as I am not, nor ever was a soldier. I was here to learn martial arts and I found some of the drilling rather frustrating as I didn't want to pretend we were in the army. At one point we were being beasted and I was doing sit-ups or crunches; my stomach muscles were screaming out but still we continued. The instructor with the dead eyes knelt beside me and started pouring water from a bottle into my face and mouth as I was doing the exercise. He was yelling at me as he did this and it was an almost out-of-body experience as I looked down at myself at the surreal vision before me where I had paid good money to be technically waterboarded.

There were a number of video clips on YouTube of this course; I have no idea if they are still up. The clips showed a few exercises that we had to do and gave a flavour of some of the training we went through. One of these was a group drill where everyone would surround one person. We would all have kick shields and would use these to crush the person as we all swarmed him as one. His job was to try to fight his way out of the crush. The feeling in the middle was not a comfortable one as your energy levels drained very quickly and breathing was hard, but you could not stop. All the while Dead Eyes would be yelling, 'Bring him to me!' in his deep, accented voice. The group would push from all sides with the pads as the man in the middle would try to clamber free; all the while the voice would be heard, 'Bring him to me!' All these years later I can still hear that voice clear as day. It's funny the things that stick in your mind.

I ended up doing several courses like this with the group over a few years and gained a great deal of knowledge from them. During that period whenever the lead instructor would visit the UK I would be on those courses. I was still pursuing training elsewhere and was running my regular classes back in Bristol, so these week-long or weekend get togethers were like a great top-up of experience. I learned a lot during that time, and it was with a heavy heart that the infighting within the group and the politics led me to move on and seek to learn elsewhere.

From little acorns

This next story is set a few years before. I had just moved again; this time I was back in the big city and wanted to continue my training in Krav Maga. I had searched around and the only group I could find ran classes out of a school hall that was situated in one of the outlying suburbs. I had been training regularly and wanted to keep that up as I was enjoying the process and had found that it fitted in well with all the previous things I had done.

The day arrived and I grabbed my training bag and drove across town to the training venue. I met the instructor who was a shortish guy with a slight frame. Softly spoken with a thinning head of hair he was a direct contrast to the physical presence of previous instructors. We greeted each other with a smile and shook hands. I was paired up with an ex-military guy and we ran through some beginner-level techniques. I remember that first day as being very warm and bright; sunlight shone through the large windows that covered three of the walls. If you turned the wrong way you were momentarily blinded by the sun. The floors were the old-style parquet flooring and they had a collection of tatty judo mats that we would get one between two.

For a few weeks this continued, and we never strayed past basic technique until one day on week four, maybe five, we were going to be shown some groundwork. Now the UFC had exploded and BJJ was gaining in popularity and so the new reality was that you should learn some ground stuff. Instantly it was obvious the instructor's knowledge in this area was limited. That was to be expected as his background was in a stand-up art before moving across to Krav. As I had done some (limited) grappling and wrestling by this point I volunteered to show a slight modification to the technique to improve it. So, in our pairs we took our positions on our judo mat and went through the motions. The modification did help and a few of the fellow trainees thanked me for sharing it.

Unfortunately, the instructor didn't feel the same way. At the end of the session he called me to one side and explained that perhaps I should look to train elsewhere. I had badly misjudged the situation.

In my previous group we worked on the premise that if someone thought they knew a better way or could add to the group knowledge it was positively encouraged to share that with everyone, thereby benefiting us all. We were a mixed bag of experiences with different backgrounds that brought together an eclectic knowledge base that would often surprise us with the results. I run the same ethos in my classes for this type of training, as the one who thinks they know everything is a special kind of stupid.

Now what's interesting about this story is that the instructor involved has gone on to build an empire. He now runs a large organisation with a very polished brand. His marketing is very good, and any naysayers are met with a barrage of online vitriol that steamrolls anyone in its path. I have no axe to grind and it has been interesting watching him grow his group, but each time I hear his name or see an ad on Facebook I think back to that sunny evening all those years ago.

All about the money.

'Gimme your f@ckin money!' Bob Geldolf might be the famous voice that offered these words out during the Live Aid concert, but the next instructor embraced this ethos also. Unfortunately all profits were for him alone.

I was on another Krav course. This one was also a week long but with a different organisation. I had seen the instructor on TV shows and read about him in magazine articles, so I had made the decision he was legit without doing any further research. The course if I remember rightly was down south. Epsom in Surrey maybe? I didn't have a car at that point so my good friends Tabbs and Simon had taken the time to drive me down. The course itself had been an expensive purchase and during the 'selection process' to attend I'd had to do a phone interview with him.

I was sat in a local pub beer garden with my then girlfriend when the call came. A thick, accented male voice asked if it was me and then introduced himself. I quickly got up from the table and walked to the end of the garden with my finger in my ear to try to hear him over the noise of the conversations going on around me. He asked for my experience, so I told him of my previous training and with whom. He asked about any criminal convictions as he said he would not take me if I had any. The irony of that statement is now frankly amazing as the person in question has been proven to be a fraud and liar and I believe is wanted in certain countries on charges. He then asked why I wanted to do this course. I gave the best answers that I could and at the end of the conversation he said I had been accepted and he would connect me to someone (I think her name was Linda) to take payment.

Again, I found myself in the position of being in a room full of strangers. This time we were in a large sports hall and were congregated in a semicircle around the edge of the mats. It was during this opening speech the he said quite clearly that he had trained directly with Imi (the founder of Krav Maga) and helped to create some of its teaching with him. This has since been disproved completely and so we were not off to the best start. Although at that time we were all unaware of the deceit and fabricated lies and half-truths used to create a history that wasn't true.

I will say now that the instructor in question was/is actually a very knowledgeable martial artist with a very solid base in Judo and some other things. If he had just stuck with that, he would have retained his credibility as his physical skills were actually very good. For the duration of the week we drilled and drilled, repeating the same core techniques. It seemed monotonous at the time but that helped to ingrain those movements into my memory.

I had booked into a local B&B that was to describe it kindly, quirky. It was run by an older lady who wore way too much make-up and had two of those dogs that looked like giant puffballs. She seemed to have at least one of them clutched in her arms at any given moment. The place was pokey with a narrow staircase that became the enemy to us all by day three. It wasn't the climbing up them at the end of the day that was the problem but coming down in the mornings. The build-up of lactic acid and the pounding the body had been through made the morning descent feel like the north face of the Eiger. It turned out that some fellow students had also booked there and everyone staying was on the course. Very quickly the hallways filled with the pungent fragrance of Tiger Balm and Deep Heat.

The owner was obviously lacking in any customer service as the moment I arrived before I had even entered the house, she stood in the doorway hand held open, demanding payment for the stay. She proved it beyond any doubt the next morning. The hours for breakfast were set for the guests, which unfortunately were too late for us as we had to get to training. As we were all at the course and the only guests we asked if it would be possible for her to supply breakfast a little earlier. Her first response was a very firm no, but we persisted. Eventually she agreed to supply breakfast for us in the most begrudging manner possible. The next morning, we awoke and stiffly descended the stairs to the dining room. There sat a number of foil parcels. The owner had made bacon sandwiches the night before and left them on the table for us. Each individual parcel held one round of sweaty, white bread which encased one rasher of bacon. Every morning was the same and the way she would glare at us made it clear we should act grateful.

The training consisted of disarms that were very different to the Krav Maga I had previously experienced. The physical skills were solid but came from a Judo bent, and I remember the striking techniques and defences to have been a little off to me, which highlighted the grappling background. Overall, I found it to be an ok course, but what I didn't like was the arrangements for progressing.

The course itself had been just shy of a thousand pounds and the certificate was dated for one year. To remain current, you would need to attend another course at another thousand pounds. There were also levels with this being the first. To progress you would need to join the next course at again, you guessed it, a thousand pounds. The cost of all these courses would soon mount up and I was not sure if I wanted to commit myself financially to such a progression route, but as luck would have it fate intervened.

After a week of solid practice and the cost of travelling, hotel rooms and outsourced breakfasts the course was drawing to a close. We had survived graduation day and passed the testing phase and were about to proudly receive our certificates. It was at this point that an assistant instructor walked across the room. In his arms he carried a large cardboard box which he put down at the feet of the instructor. Without pausing the instructor reached down, opened the box and pulled out some branded t-shirts. After all the money spent and effort put in the words that came out of his mouth were a metaphorical kick in the balls. He said, 'You can buy a t-shirt from us for £15'.

I was honestly amazed that he was trying to wring another few quid out of us after all that. In fact, I was more than amazed, I was fucking annoyed. That £15 for me was the straw that broke the camel's back and I never did another of those courses. Over time the truth as regards his history started to come out and the things he had claimed were disproved.

As Simon and Tabbs pulled up in the jeep I climbed into the back seat. The entire journey home was spent being jumped on and tea bagged by an over excited staffy while I pondered on what I was going to try next.

Sport v's street.

This time I was off to London for more training. I was sat in the passenger seat with a fellow student I vaguely knew driving. I had been picked up from the outskirts of Bristol where I had left my car to the mercy of the locals. He had borrowed his father-in-law's people carrier for a few days to get us there. Once again, I had signed up for yet another Krav course, and once again it was with yet another organisation. These guys claimed to teach an outside-the-chip-shop type Krav that had a very UK flavour.

We drove down to the gym, getting confused on the way as the sat nav suddenly went dark. We pondered what that could mean as it was the first time either of us had used one as we finally found the venue. On going inside, we found a pretty cramped training space in a fully working fighters' gym. At one end was a MMA cage with a sign that read, 'Please do not feed the animals,' stuck to the side. Kick shields and Thai pads lined the walls and there was a large tractor tyre in the corner.

We were introduced to our instructors; one was a fit-looking guy of middling years and greying hair in a short military style buzz cut He had a very heavy regional accent and a forthright manner. The second was a younger man; he was from Brazil with an olive-skinned athletically muscled body. He was a world champion BJJ competitor and I remember his movements as being very smooth and deceptively light. His grip was vicelike, and the strength of the man far outweighed the proportions of his physical frame.

The training began and we had done a few hours, I had a few questions in my mind as to the validity of some of the techniques outside of a sporting arena and had chatted to my mate about it in the break. He felt similar, but we decided to stick with it as both instructors were knowledgeable people. We then moved onto some knife defence and this is where I lost all faith. The BJJ instructor had just performed an amazing jumping armbar where he leapt into the air turning almost upside down as he went, throwing his legs around the head and shoulders of the knife-wielding attacker. It was then hanging upside down he hyperextended the elbow joint and locked in the armbar. The technique was a thing of beauty performed by a master of his craft. Unfortunately, the skills required to pull that off smoothly against an armed opponent in a real life or death scenario were well beyond me and my fellow trainees, and a few hours' training would not make us proficient enough to even think about trying to use it. I had been seeking simple, effective, workable techniques that I could perform under stress with as little personal risk as possible. This technique was the polar opposite, and was almost suicidal if it was anything less than 100% perfect. You were upside down, main arteries were exposed, the attacker was carrying your weight; there was no easy release. To me, although an amazing example of skill and dexterity, it was not a technique I could look at seriously as something to consider against a knife.

My friend and I exchanged glances with raised eyebrows and shrugs. At the next break we spoke briefly. There was no need for a long-drawn-out conversation; we had both seen enough to tell us this was not the course for us. As we didn't want to waste any more time with training we were not happy with, and being rather disappointed, we decided to just get in the car and leave. The drive back was a mixture of confusion as we analysed the small part of the course we had done. It was odd as both instructors had vast knowledge and skillsets, and from what I could gather both had been around some tough situations, so I was expecting the system they were promoting to be far more usable than I found it to be.

I enjoyed my years doing Krav and KAPAP and for a few years even ran my KAPAP Bristol group from the old Sweatbox gym in Bristol. I do not claim to be an expert or instructor in either now, as the face of Krav is changing so rapidly it is almost unrecognisable from what it was fifteen to twenty years ago.

The Sweatbox did exactly what it said on the tin. Years ago, it was located on a pedestrianised street covering two floors above a travel agent. Narrow stairs led up to the first floor where a fully matted area opened up. It was small with barred windows at one end and a pile of rag tag bags and pads in the corner. Upstairs was another room with a ring and a few hanging bags. On one wall was a mirror with a large crack along the bottom. A changing room stood off to one side and the whole space felt crowded if you had ten people in the room. There was a mixture of classes going on from Thai boxing to BJJ to western boxing to Capoeira. I had two classes a week on a Saturday afternoon and a Wednesday evening. On Saturdays we followed the Capoeira class and often would turn up in time to watch the beautiful dance they would perform as they twirled and span, the rhythmic music setting time. Once a month the stick fighters would come in and we would have to go upstairs where my guys would take advantage of the ring. It was a great little gym that smelled of hard work and sweat, and it was here that one of my students achieved fame on a national scale.

Tony had been training with me for a while. He was a smiley guy in his early thirties who worked as a salesman in his day job. He was not a natural fighter which I'm sure he won't mind me saying but would train regularly on a Wednesday. He rarely did Saturdays as that class was mostly filled with off-duty doormen all standing six feet plus with bulging biceps. By his own admission it was a bit rough for him.

There was a show on Channel 4 that was very popular called *Come Dine With Me*. It was a show where complete strangers would hold dinner parties for each other. The gold of the show was the voiceover guy. He was funny and very cutting in his observations which would compel people to watch in their millions. Tony had signed up as a contestant and they wanted to do some filming in the gym.

Waivers signed, windows taped up and cameras ready to roll, we shot for around five hours to get probably a minute of screen time in the show. You can clearly see me dumping him on his butt in the ring as part of his personal introduction in the programme. They portrayed him as this oily, smug kind of guy which I know is not true. I actually cautioned him about this during the filming as you could tell by the questions, they were leading him to act a certain way. Tony didn't care though and jumped into the week with both feet. The episodes with him in it were really funny to watch, and I must try and find them again for memories' sake.

17, THERE'S NEVER A DAMSEL IN DISTRESS WHEN YOU NEED ONE.

The time I became Sir Matt, the brave and noble knight.

My journey, nay Quest began on a fantastically sunny Saturday afternoon. It was summertime and I had almost forgotten what rain felt like. Today was glorious, way too nice to stay in, so I texted a friend.

I have known my mate Wayne since we were kids. We drank together and went to concerts; we even shared some of the same bedsits. He is always great fun and his particular view on the world never fails to crack me up. So, it was him I called to see if he wanted to come along.

I now live on the South Wales border in a very picturesque part of the world that belies its bloodthirsty and gruesome history. It was here where the lines were drawn, and many men died. The border between England and Wales is separated by a series of castles. Some of these castles are mere skeletons of their former selves; crumbling walls and mounds of earth give clues to the majesty of what they once were. Others still stand proud and virtually intact, looming up out of the horizon and creating a protective shadow over the town below.

Today there was a medieval fair and re-enactment at one of the castles. Caldicot to be exact. This castle is an imposing structure with big, solid doors that open out into a well-manicured courtyard. It is surrounded by the embankments that used to hold the moat, and further out the grounds offer dog walkers and ramblers lots of places to explore. This afternoon the courtyard was full of people; all the stalls and stands were manned by hobbyists in period dress as the general public milled about. Children were excitedly asking questions and trying to touch everything in sight; others were trying the archery or putting on the helmets that some kindly middle-aged women in costume were looking after.

The tannoy announced that the battle would be starting shortly which meant that it was time to go and find a vantage point to watch from. Lots of families were here and buggies and toddlers were strewn around like litter along the edges of the roped-off field. We found a spot where we could see, but far enough away from the screeching free-range kids of the progressive parents and settled in for the show.

At first the distant sound of drums could be heard on the wind. I wondered if this was how a real battle would have begun, sitting with your fellow soldiers listening as the slow rhythmic beating resonated, stick met skin and feet marched. The drums slowly got louder as the advancing army grew ever closer. Then they came into view; re-enactors resplendent in the uniforms of the day marched side by side in rows towards the battleground. But then from the other side of the castle came the opposing force, equally as impressive in their colours.

The two sides filed towards the arena and began to filter out into battle formation. The man on the tannoy explained what was happening in that crackly, can't-really-make-it-out tannoy voice as the two sides crashed together in a series of loud roars and clanking armour. As this was a re-enactment and it was actually Fred the myopic accountant fighting Sidney who had an ingrowing toenail and enjoyed his allotment, this meant the fighting was not exactly furious. One by one in the prescribed fashion they would howl and throw themselves to the floor in their overacted death throes that reminded me of some premiership footballers. The plot had been written long ago and the history books had provided the spoilers. This was organised mayhem and a nice cup of tea awaited the victors.

But then things got really interesting for me.

We had reached the interval in the battle and Tannoy Man told us that we would now see some full contact fighting in armour. Tannoy Man shut up as a tall, skinny man walked into the open. He had long grey hair swept back in a ponytail and held a wooden staff. He screamed old hippy and when he spoke into the microphone his manner was theatrical and engaging. With arms spread wide he announced the group.

Now these guys looked completely different to the polished pomposity that had gone before. Here was a ragtag bunch in mismatched armour. None of it was gleaming and the dents and knocks in them stood out for all to see. The weapons didn't glisten, and these things looked business-like. The way they were hefted by the armoured knights told me they were not the toys we had been watching, but serious, ugly instruments of death capable of crushing injuries.

Wizard Guy explained that this was a sport and people competed in it. Unlike what we had just seen this was not scripted and the fighting would be very real. He told us that the weapons were real with the edges dulled. You can hit each other full force with them, and the trauma caused can and has led to serious injury. Some had axes, other swords and shields, one or two had polearms which are seven to eight feet long with axe blades on the end. There were no feathers or adornments on the armour; functionality was key. Although one guy had a Mohican-style plume on his helmet and carried a vicious looking battle axe with a smaller hand axe tucked into his belt. I later learned his name was Moose and by god could he throw that thing around.

The fighting began and these guys were not holding back. You could feel the impact across the field as sword met helmet, and axe met breastplate. The noise of a full contact blow hitting armour rang out and the concussive nature of the swing impacting was obvious for all to see. This was not pretend in the sense that they were taking it easy; these guys were friends but right now genuinely looked like mortal enemies.

Suddenly two of the combatants locked shields; they had clashed together, losing ground as they grasped hold of each other for purchase. Almost instantly one of the knights tilted his head back and launched a monster of a headbutt which he then followed up with two more. His opponent obviously staggered by the assault dropped to a knee. A big *ooooh!* circled around the audience as mothers quickly tried to shield their babies' eyes. 'Don't worry,' shouted the wizard as he waved his arms around. 'Headbutts are perfectly legal in our sport'.

The sport is called HMB - Historical Medieval Battles.

Right then I knew I had to have a go!

When I got back, I found myself Googling this newfound wonder and to my amazement there was a proper world championship called the Battle of the Nations. And people took it very seriously indeed. I quickly learned that as with everything politics had reared its ugly head and there were two main groups for this. The ones I had seen were called the UK Feds, the original full-contact medieval combat group, so those were the ones I wanted to follow up with. As luck would have it, they were holding an open training session the very next weekend in Nottingham at their HQ at a farm. As I had already decided that I wanted to try it, it was an easy decision to get in the car and drive up.

Welcome to the Buhurt

I arrived at the farm to be given a very warm welcome. The HQ is just outside Nottingham and the land is attached to a working crop farm with a delightful farm shop that sells amazing fresh produce and has a lovely café. It was such a great feeling to go in and sit by the fire as your toes defrosted after training. After following the track down, I found the training area and the place where I would be pitching my tent. People were already on site and there was quite a lot of activity.

I was introduced to a number of people, all with great names like Badger and Kurgan. They were all a bit of a blur to be honest but the one that sticks in my mind is a guy called Gruff. It will become obvious why very soon. Gruff was a well-built strong stocky guy with wild, curly hair and a beard that was greying when we met. The name was not a reflection on character as he was a lovable guy with a ready smile and a mischievous glint in his eye. When I met him, life was kicking him around a bit, but I never saw that dampen his spirit. He would help me to figure out what I needed to know and was even kind enough to loan me his armour on more than one occasion. Buying a suit of armour is not a cheap thing. You have to use the materials from the period, and it has to be of a quality good enough to withstand full-contact blows. It also needs to be tailored individually to the person otherwise you can barely move. As I was new to this, I had no kit or weapons and so relied on the kindness of the group.

Now the point of the group is to fight, so it was time to get kitted up and try it out. Wearing a full suit of armour is an interesting thing. You cannot get dressed alone and putting it on is a two-person job. Everything has a very specific way of going together and once enclosed in it you heat up very quickly. Movement is limited and the suits do weight a lot. But all of that is of no consequence when the helmet is lowered onto your head. The first urge is to panic; it's not normal to be enclosed like that and the feeling of being trapped is very real. Next you notice your breathing. Due to the protective nature of the helmet both sight and breathing are impaired. Every inhale and exhale is echoed in the space and it seems like your heart is on the outside by the noise it's making.

I remember thinking: how in the world did knights of old wear this stuff day in and day out in all climates and weather conditions? Just walking around in the armour is incredibly tiring, never mind fighting a battle for hours or marching for days. But these guys were the lucky ones as most could not afford armour and so had to make do with what they had.

Now that I had tried on the suit it was time to practise. For this we had light padded armour similar to the riot gear Police use. We were issued wooden weapons and bucklers which are small, rounded shields which are great to use as giant knuckledusters. Then we were introduced to the Buhurt. This is a square piece of ground where the combat takes place. This one was surrounded by thick, wooden poles to keep the action in. We were ushered into teams of five and told to go to our side of the arena. As I stood there with my cohort, I could see Gruff stood with his team. We were all eager and bounced from foot to foot as adrenaline raced through us. This was what I had come for, not the history or the costume, but the battle. As the flag was dropped, we ran towards each other to engage, furiously hacking and slashing at anyone close enough. The older hands had some tactics and were looking to strategically pick off their enemies one by one. As the melee continued, I got engaged with an opponent and we grappled together in the corner. Held up by the wooden posts neither one of us would give quarter. It was then I felt a massive blow to my head. Gruff had come to support his teammate and hit me with the pummel of the sword, opening up a crescent-shaped gash on the top of my head that instantly started bleeding. I grabbed hold of him and by luck more than skill managed to bring both combatants to the floor with me as I fell. The rules are last man standing and if you hit the floor you are out. So, to take two with me was a good thing.

Blood was steadily pumping from my head as we went off to find a bandage to fix it up. Once it was cleaned and dressed, I stuck my helmet back on and re-entered the fray. That attitude went down well with the group who are all a little bit bonkers. By the end of the training session I had angry purple and black welts running the length of my right leg, a deep cut to my head and a golf ball-sized swelling to top it off. I wanted to do it again of course.

18, 'BOING!' SAID ZEBEDEE.

I am not one of those naturally bouncy people who leap about like a lizard on hot sand. I have always been more of a solid, stable type, able to move quickly when I need to, but preferring to stay somewhat connected to the ground. However, I have always admired the athleticism and gymnastic ability of the tricksters and Tae Kwon Do exponents. Are these moves any use in a real fight? Who cares when you can just admire then for the perfection of physical skill that they are?

If we remember right back at the start of my story, I told of a young boy who wanted to kick more than anything. As the years passed and the type of training required for me and my work role changed, I had moved away from the arts that weren't instantly usable for me. Now at no point am I saying that high kicks, spinning kicks and any kind of jump kick won't work in a fight as there are people out there who can make them work. But they are the exception to the rule, and more often than not kicking range is either never there or lost in an instance.

I had found myself at a Tae Kwon Do club in Newport. Firstly, I was going to support a friend who trained there, but over time I wanted to know more about the style. The group were a great bunch of people and they ran a very successful club with many champions in the ranks. Some of these guys had amazing skills with their kicks and it was a pleasure to watch them work. The kicks of TKD are not the same as Karate, kickboxing or Thai boxing and I was very interested in learning how to perform them. Whenever I see something new or different, I want to try to understand it and break it down to see if I can add it to what I do.

Coming from my background the basic kicks were not that dissimilar so I could perform these with relative ease. I have always maintained a reasonable level of flexibility and kicking to head height has never been a problem. What was a problem is that this level wasn't even close to the flexibility required to perform some of these techniques. Did I mention strength? Turns out I am pretty strong, but nowhere near strong enough to lift my legs with the control required. This is always one of the great things about stepping outside your immediate art. It stretches you and tests what you take for granted.

My hosts were very gracious and took the time to help me with this. In return I would take their students and show them what I did so they could add that to their mix. Being a black belt in other things kicking-related meant that coming in as a white belt should have been a difficult thing for my ego to overcome, but it was quite the opposite. The group acknowledged my experience in my field, and I was happy to acknowledge theirs. In fact, it was this knowledge-sharing principle that had led me to my current position.

I was at the end of a long garden; large conifer type trees blocked off the road that ran alongside. As I bounced up and down on the large kids' trampoline, I could see the neighbour doing the washing up through her kitchen window. I was with a fourth-degree world champion blackbelt in Tae Kwon Do, and in return for teaching him some of my skills he was going to help me progress with some of the more flamboyant kicks. We had done a warm-up on his patio which was pretty standard with some pad drills and cardio. We had broken out the BOB (Human torso-shaped punch bag) and started to work on the turning kicks and some specific exercises to help build explosive movement in the legs. He had a wall around two feet high that ran along one edge of the patio, that we used to do repeated sets of box jumps until the muscles were sore. We then ran through a stretching routine when the muscles were warm to get maximum benefit which lasted maybe twenty minutes. Even the stretching seemed like hard work, and several of the positions were alien to me, but there is no denying the positive results as he could kick with speed, precision and power.

We were now working on the 360 tornado kick. This is a jumping spinning kick where you whip your back leg around as you jump in the air. You then do a full turn and kick with the other leg. You can add turns onto this to make it more difficult and the really good guys will spin three or four times in mid-air. We had been working on this and his instruction had gotten me this far, which meant I could perform the movement, but it just wasn't gelling as a whole.

This is where he suggested we head down the garden. As I followed down the path past the shed and tangle of kids bikes that were piled against it, I saw a large kids' trampoline. It was one of those big, round ones with a safety net around it. It stood around three foot off the floor and was maybe eight foot across. Scattered across the canvas were kids' toys including a stuffed rabbit and at least two footballs. He swept these away and with a broad smile told me to get up. He stood there looking at me with his arms folded as I self-consciously gave a few test bounces. I couldn't remember the last time I had been on a trampoline and memories of *You've Been Framed* clips came flooding back as I gingerly felt the spring of the material under my feet.

'Bounce higher!' he shouted up between chuckles, so I did. This was when the neighbour doing her dishes was met with my head appearing over the horizon as I reached the top of my jump. Our eyes locked as I disappeared back down from view only to reappear again on the up part of the next jump. This time the neighbour became fixated on the soapy mugs and refused to look up again, probably wondering to herself what the hell I was doing. What I was doing was learning to jump as the next command was to spin in mid-air. Every time I went up, I was to turn full circle to land balanced. 'This is how I learned to do it,' he told me as once again my attempts were met with a loss of balance and an ungainly landing. Every time I faceplanted the trampoline, I would hear a laugh, and the words, 'Do it again.'

This was how I learned to perform some of the jump spinning kicks. I do not claim expertise, and whatever skill I once possessed in this has slowly dwindled away through old age and injury, although unlike a lot of my fellow practitioners I haven't needed hip replacements yet. For those that know me personally the idea of me jumping up and down on that trampoline may seem silly, but it was actually a great aid to learning how to accomplish the movement.

Now if only I could find an easy way to remember the Korean.

19, A LESSON IN HUMILITY.

It was one of those days where I had not planned it to work out this way, but it had, and my ego was placed firmly back in its box. Through a distinct lack of organisational skills and a certain amount of luck I had found myself in the position where I had two serious training sessions on the same day. My life at the time had very little continuity to it, so scheduling anything could prove quite tough. In between teaching, training, working the doors and holding down my day job as an operations manager, my free time was sporadic and limited. It changed daily and quite often would change in the moment as the phone would go and I would have to charge off and firefight something.

So, the only time we could all make the sessions was today. This morning was my first session and it was with a multiple world champion points fighter. He was a lovely guy, tall with a lean, muscular physique. He kept in tip-top condition and was extremely fit. I arrived at his gym and we exchanged pleasantries while I got changed. We did some warm-up drills and had a good stretch before moving on to some padwork. Once all this was out of the way the point of the session was upon us. This was to spar. We had agreed that we were going to get a good few rounds in during the time we had.

Being a points fighter meant his range was longer than mine and carrying at least three stone less than me while only conceding an inch in height meant he had speed as well. Hi movement was elusive, and it was like trying to punch smoke or nail jelly to a wall. He would be out of range bouncing on the balls of his feet and then move in with rapid fire combinations disappearing again before I could retaliate. I would flail my arms at where he used to be. My footwork seemed cumbersome compared to his, and my own attacks met fresh air as he would backpeddle out of range. I decided to change tack and try to cut him off; obviously allowing him all this movement was to his advantage. I started stalking him, cutting down the space and not allowing him the angles to move; once cornered I could land some shots of my own - but almost as soon as I had closed him down, he was gone again. His punches and kicks were sharp and accurate, and as they were not looking to penetrate in the way full contact shots do, he was always at the edge of his reach peppering me with combinations. I would cover and throw back, but in reality, I was outgunned in this style of fighting. Sweat dripped from me from the exertion and the explosive pace we had been keeping. Round after round I had lost on points as he had definitely landed more shots than me.

Not to worry I told myself; if it really mattered, I would jump on him and drag his arse to the floor where I would choke him out. He wouldn't be able to stand up to my grappling, and so like a toddler with a comfort blanket I held onto this thought to make me feel more secure with myself.

There was time for a shower and lunch before it was back in the car to drive across town to another gym for my second appointment of the day. This time I was already dressed in shorts and t-shirt. My meeting was with a semi-pro MMA fighter who had done a lot of BJJ and had been a private student for years of one of the best professors in the UK. We had agreed to meet and have an open mat session where we would just roll and see where it took us.

I walked in to find him already sat on the mats. Dressed in MMA shorts and a rashguard with a thin sheen of perspiration covering his brow he had obviously been using the time to warm up as he waited for me. We chatted for a few minutes as I limbered up and ran through some warm-up drills. He was an interesting guy with many fingers in many pies, and my guess is that some of them may have sailed a little close to the wind. Moving a little more freely now we decided to get on with it. We faced each other on our knees, slapped hands and bumped knuckles as our way of acknowledging each other and thanking each other for the opportunity to train and learn. We engaged in a little light grip fighting to test each other out and see how we moved, feinting in to force an overreaction, and testing each other's balance.

He was significantly lighter than me and for the second time today I was being handled with ease. It is one thing to know how to apply a figure four or Kimura on an unresisting, compliant opponent. It is quite another to apply those techniques on a skilled opponent who is trying to do the same to you. Even with my size and strength advantage I was having a hard time applying anything; worse still the openings I thought I saw were actually traps, set to lull me in. Tap, tap, tap. My hand hit the mat three times in rapid succession as the armbar was applied and my elbow joint was being manipulated against its natural movement. He raised his hips slightly to take away any slack in the technique and my hyperextended arm was at the end of its range of movement. I had to tap right now or suffer the risk of serious injury. This is why you must have trust in your partner and the tap agreement.

I lost count of the number of submissions he applied on me. I also have conveniently forgotten how many I managed to pull off on him. It is enough to say his offer of calling it a draw was an act of kindness bordering on pity. We had been rolling for nearly two hours straight and for the second time today I was left soaked in sweat and soundly outclassed by a smaller guy.

But it's ok, I told myself; I would punch him long before he could take me down. My footwork and movement were too good; my angles and use of range would make it impossible for him to get me down, and I would pick him off with kicks if he tried. If this had been for real, I wouldn't have let him get close enough to grab me!

This was the second lie of the day that I told myself and it gave me comfort to believe it.

How many times have we seen this exact thought process? The grappler tells himself that he will shoot on the striker and get past the strikes with ease, in the same way the striker will claim to be able to maintain striking distance while picking off the grappler with strikes. This day happened to me many years ago and yet I still see people spout this on Facebook.

I went home a little dejected as I was a seasoned martial artist and bouncer. I had won competitions and bar fights alike and had an inflated self of my own capabilities. But that is exactly why I had instigated days like today. I had to find out where I was strong and weak, who had the best knowledge and what was going to suit me. My too-deadly street-lethal combative type training was great, and I won't dismiss it, but without live training with very capable people who are experts in their fields you will never know how effective that type of training really is. Today I had found out where the gaps were, and once I had taken a short while to wallow in my own misery, it was time to thank them for helping me to figure out what I needed to learn to make my personal skillset better.

PART 4.
FULL CIRCLE

When we come full circle there is a feeling that we have come to a familiar place, but we are somehow different.

And the end of all our exploring / Will be to arrive where we started / And know the place for the first time -

TS Eliot – 'Little Gidding'

20, MY OWN PLACE.

The time had come. I had been teaching out of other people's facilities for a number of years and although grateful to each of them for the opportunity, it was time to move on and think bigger.

One of the places I used to teach in was called the Sweatbox in Bristol run by Jess and John. This was an old facility above a travel agent. The gym itself was over two floors. You accessed them by climbing a narrow flight of stairs. The first level was a matted room with large windows on the end wall that were barred and looked down over the pedestrianised shopping area below. The second floor held bags and a ring. The area was cramped and alongside it sat the changing rooms.

On Saturday afternoons at two o'clock I would run a class. Back then we were called KAPAP Bristol, and the class was 99% doormen and bouncers. Very large men were the norm in those sessions, and we had a lot of fun doing those. All of the guys joining in wanted workable skills as quickly as possible, so the classes were very rough and tumble with a lot of free sparring and testosterone. You had to have a certain disposition to take part.

We also did a Wednesday class there which was a little more technical and attracted a slightly different demographic. No less enthusiastic in the approach, but a little more cautious with regards to just how far they wanted to push the boundaries.

Another place I ran classes for a while was the Urban Gym run by Scott. Situated just off a roundabout on a busy road in Bristol, this was a great little space with a low ceiling and good energy. You went downstairs to access this one, and at the bottom of the stairs the matted area opened out to create an intimate training area. One of my memories of that time was when a black belt friend of a student came to train.

My student was a young nineteen-year-old who worked as a doorman and had a history of Judo. He was a heavyset guy, solid and powerful and liked to mix it up. He had been telling his friend about our classes and the things that we did. His friend trained in another system. A very well-recognised style of practice that had both traditional and sporting aspects to it. He was very much of the style and felt quite strongly that his training would carry him through any street altercation he may encounter. Predominantly a kicker with a very unrealistic view as to his punching capabilities and zero grappling skills we felt that one of these classes might offer a little enlightenment as to the holes in his knowledge.

The drill was simple. A basic pressure test involving punching. Only four punches are allowed, and gloves are a must. The idea is to defend the punches and control your posture. The puncher is trying to take advantage of any gaps or overreactions. Within seconds the friend had turned sideways on and curled into a foetal position covering his head with his hands in the most submissive posture possible. We had spent the past thirty minutes of class teaching him the finer points of this drill, but when we reran it the same thing happened. My green belts were overwhelming this guy with ease, and he had nothing to answer them with.

All misconceptions of his perceived ability exposed he was left with two stark choices. Learn from the experience, adapt his training methodology and improve, or take option two which is what he did. We never saw him in one of my classes again. Instead he had gone back to his club and in the safety bubble of style convinced himself it never happened. A year or so down the line I was both amused and appalled to see him advertising classes that promised self-defence.

Bodybuilder and the powerslap

Another class I used to run was a hired hall in a franchise fitness gym. This catered for all things Lycra, from CrossFitters with their holier-than-thou attitude right through to the Dairylea Triangle-type bodybuilder; you know the one. Five foot seven tall, to overcompensate for his stature he packs on so much muscle mass he looks just like one of those Dairylea Triangles. It was one of these guys that was watching us now. I had only been running the class for a few short weeks and had maybe half a dozen complete beginners in the session. We were in one of the fitness studios where along one wall ran full length mirrors; along the other ran a balcony that was home to a selection of weightlifting machines. This was where the human triangle stood. Rocking one of those vests they always wear where there is always at least one nipple exposed, and grasping the obligatory protein shake, he was glaring down on us from above, and even without any words being spoken you just knew he was dismissing everything he had seen.

It always makes me wonder why people do this, as I see it time and time again. Martial artists dismiss other styles and fitness groups claim superiority over all others. This guy seemed to think that because he could lift heavy things up and struggled to find jeans that would fit, he was Hercules reincarnated. Disdain wafted from him like a fragrance as I tried my best to ignore both him and the silly stare he was projecting our way.

As this was a beginners' group I was showing some very basic open hand strikes which while being safer for the hands are also psychologically easier to throw for the novice. Punching someone in the face or instigating violence against an aggressor is actually very hard for a lot of people. The strike of choice at the moment was a powerslap. I had seen many versions of this over the years but Master Dave Turton's still remains one of the best. I had explained to them a few variants such as impact points on the hand and various target areas along the high line of the head. I had explained the need to not telegraph the shot and how to generate force with the hips. Talking over it was time to try it on the pads. The students partnered up and with varying degrees of success begin to hit the focus mitts.

Meanwhile Dairylea Dan had made his way down the stairs and was heading our way with the gait of a man who had forgotten to take the clothes hanger out of his t-shirt. He marched up to me and puffed out his chest to try and take the emphasis off the fact he had to look up to me. 'Bitch slapping someone like that won't do shit,' he confidently announced to me. Trying to be as diplomatic as possible as it was a new venue with new students I replied with, 'It's a strong shot when performed correctly; maybe you'd like to join us and learn it?' 'I would punch your fucking head in if you tried that on me,' came the charming response. Aware that he was purposely trying to create a confrontation and knowing that given the abnormal size of his arms he couldn't punch anyone unless they stood still and let him, I figured this might just be a great learning moment for the group. I gave him my best Clint Eastwood face and told him to fuck off back to sticking needles in his arse.

As expected, he threw a haymaker with no style or technique. Watching him wind it up was like watching an ocean liner try to turn. As I was pretty sure this exact thing was going to happen, I had casually positioned myself behind my short non-aggressive stance and lined him up for the shot. He had no idea this was happening, so great was his own confidence. The powerslap I threw connected clean long before there was any danger of his shot landing. It made a satisfactory thwacking noise as hand met head and the concussive nature of the blow sent him toppling to the floor. It didn't quite knock him out, but he staggered around like Bambi on ice for best part of thirty seconds before starting to regain his composure. I told him to go away before I really hit him and went back to the class. As a group they were all very vocal in their excitement at what had just happened, and I must admit to having a quiet smile to myself as Dairylea Dan had just done more to promote my class than a thousand leaflets could.

Was I being overconfident in my belief that I could get to him first? No, as he was so over-muscled, he had lost a lot of range of movement. He had also lost speed if he ever had any, and I knew his arrogance would mean he would not be looking for any kind of defence. Couple that with his obvious lack of fighting prowess when he opened his arms wide and thrust his chest forward in a brilliant display of innocence. Also, as he had been so bold in his verbal attacks, he had really forced my hand. My new students would not stay students for long if I had swallowed that from him. Of course, they would have nodded and agreed that I was the bigger man if I had left it, but afterwards they would realise they had lost respect and confidence in me. Within a few short weeks they would have all been gone. Maybe Dairylea Dan knew this and maybe not. Either way it was one more reason to try to find my own place.

I had made the decision to take the leap and try and find my own gym. It was going to be a big leap, but one I felt ready for. I scoured around for a while and found a few maybes, but nothing really seemed ideal for what I wanted. Then one day a friend mentioned I should try a local businessman who owned a lot of industrial properties in the area and also across the UK. I immediately jumped in the car and drove around to one of the shops they owned and asked to speak to the owner.

Five minutes later my phone started to ring. He said he had a property I might like. I took the address from him as I juggled the phone under my chin by holding it in place with my shoulder while I scribbled the address on a scrap of paper. As he told me where it was my heart rate quickened a little and a strange feeling came over me.

I drove straight to the property and stood looking out at a view that years ago totally changed the shape of my world. Whether it was fate or just some sort of weird luck I don't know, but as I stood there looking out through the large double metal gates my eyes fell on the very spot my father had been found dead many years before.

My Dad was a large, heavy-drinking man known for violence. He worked dirty, manual jobs all his life and on his knuckles were homemade tattoos of his nickname, Spud. In those days being a man meant you didn't talk about your feelings and you certainly didn't admit weakness to your friends. You would grab a pint, say something sarcastic, and move on. Talking about emotions was not a man's man thing to do, and my Dad was certainly that.

He had married my Mum and they went on to have two children, myself being the older and a sister two years younger. Life was hard and the arguments were many. Finally, after several years they divorced leaving us with Mum and a very sporadic relationship with my father. He would often disappear for months and we would wait at the window, convinced he would show up even through history had proved us wrong countless times in the past. Mum bore the brunt of this, as our childhood anger at this had to go somewhere, and Dad wasn't around.

When he did show up though, everything was forgotten in that instant and once again he was my hero, the larger than life figure that would pile us in the car and off we would go on a mini adventure for a few hours. I don't know who was at fault or the forces at play during that time and I am not going to speculate, but eventually Dad met another woman whom he later married. They too had two children. A daughter followed by a son came along as did a new house and a new life. Begrudgingly my new stepmum acknowledged my sister's and my existence, but it was with a constant look of distaste in her mouth. I think it is fair to say we never liked one another.

My assessment of her proved correct when she chose to have an affair. Dad worked all hours to bring money in and she was a lot younger. I guess boredom got the better of her and her eyes drifted to someone a little more exciting. When my father found out he was devastated. I remember him at that time and the strong man I knew had been brought to his knees by this. He would sit, hour after hour at the kitchen table staring at nothing. The only noise would be the rustle as he opened yet another packet of cigarettes and the low chatter from the sitting room where everyone but him would sit. All the memories of the happy years swimming around his head as his mind slowly ate him away from the inside.

He ended up staying with my sister in the spare room while we looked for a flat that we could share together. He was quiet and morose, and his normal quick smile seemed a lifetime away, but I never expected what happened next.

I was in my bedsit when the doorbell rang. I could hear muffled talking in the hallway followed by a knock on my room door. I lived in a shared house at the time and my room had a single bed and a chair in it. We shared the kitchen and toilet and seeing how long we could survive without washing up was the order of the day. I got off my bed and opened the door to be met with two police officers, a man and a woman. With them was my uncle and all of them were stern-faced as they asked me to sit down. My first thought was that my Dad had been arrested for something, but that wasn't it. 'I am really sorry, but your Dad is dead,' the male copper said to me. The room was small at the best of times and felt crowded with all these bodies in it. It seemed like there was no air left in the room as I tried to process those words. I couldn't or wouldn't acknowledge the statement in that moment so instead I offered them a cup of tea. Of course, they refused, but I didn't know what else to do.

I looked at the bedside table with the ripped Rizla packet and bits of stray tobacco strewn over it. I wondered if the police had noticed the dogends with the roaches in the ashtray, the remnants from last night's joint. If they had noticed they didn't mention it as they tried to offer words of comfort that were falling on deaf ears. I have always wondered how it must feel to tell a stranger that a loved one is dead. But not then; right then I just wanted them to leave.

My Dad had gone out and acquired all the things needed to carry out his plan. Telling no one of his thoughts he arranged to meet some old friends for a drink that night. According to them he was chatty and drunk but made no mention of what he had planned for that night. He said his goodbyes and left with them none the wiser, to make his way to the car that was parked around the back of the club. He had parked it there so he wouldn't be disturbed as it was out of sight of the main road and no one should be walking around that time of night. Knowing Dad, he had a fag hanging out of his mouth while he did this; he fed the hosepipe from the exhaust into the driver's side window which would allow the silent killer of the fumes to do their work. He taped up all the windows so it would be airtight and nothing would escape. This must have taken a little time, but he was obviously set on his path because he got into the car, turned on the ignition and waited to sleep knowing he would never wake again.

He was found early in the morning the next day by a paperboy on his rounds. The deed was done, and his planning had paid off. My father was dead, and my cramped bedsit was the setting where I was told.

The property overlooked the very carpark where this happened and when I opened the doors the view framed within them showed me the exact spot. Some may say that it is not a view they would want, but for me it means something very different. It was like it was a message direct from the dead. That view reminds me every day to do the best I can. It tells me that whatever the problem is it can be overcome. It tells me to live my life to the maximum. And finally, it reminds me of the most important man in my life and what a great guy he was. Yes, he had his faults, but I remember him every day not as an old man, grown weary with age, but young, vibrant, and strong. Time passes but he remains constant. The view is a reminder of that.

21, STUDENTS.

It's always interesting to see the different people and how they react to the training. Retelling the stories of a few of them I hope will help to give a sense of why I teach and train the way that I do.

Have you ever heard an instructor say that something will work on everyone?

I have, and it made no sense to me then, in the same way as it makes no sense now. My advice is that if you ever meet an instructor who say something will work 100% of the time against 100% of people, smile politely and walk away. You have just met an idiot.

I am going to introduce you to one of my students, who had a super-power, although it came at a great cost.

He first walked into my gym a few years ago as a thin-framed guy with tattoos up his arms in sleeves and short grey hair. He would always be sporting a t-shirt with one heavy metal band or another on it. He had done some martial arts before and had a background in one of the Chinese systems. He asked if he could train but said he had some very specific issues we would need to be aware of.

About a year before he had been involved in a terrible car accident. He told me he had been renovating an old sports car, the type that didn't have power steering or ABS brakes. He had spent a lot of time and love on the project until he was able to enjoy the fruits of his labour. He had been driving along a country road when suddenly there was a problem in front of him. They had rounded a bend in the road to meet a queue of cars. He tried to brake and threw the steering wheel around in a vain attempt to avoid a collision. It was too late and he ploughed into another car, killing the occupants of the vehicle and sustaining life-threatening injuries himself.

He was found innocent of any wrongdoing and the accident was deemed to be just that, an accident. However during the time it took to go through the courts, the threat of prison was very real and the feelings of guilt at the death of those people weighed heavily on him. He blamed himself and sometimes his thoughts were very dark. He readily admits that he was in a bad way mentally.

Physically he was also suffering. His skull was held together by titanium plates and he'd had numerous surgeries including facial reconstruction procedures. He'd been in a coma after the crash and barely pulled through himself, leaving him with very serious, life-changing injuries.

One of the other things that happened as part of the damage sustained by his brain was that his neural pathways were somehow interrupted, and his pain receptors were faulty. In layman's terms, he felt no pain. You could stab him with a fork or stamp on his foot or even apply an armbar until it snapped, and he would just look at you blankly. Pain compliance techniques had no effect whatsoever and any kind of body manipulation through the use of joints was redundant. He presented an interesting challenge with regards to making things work on him individually.

We understand that pain is our friend and it is there to save us from our own stupidity, and having a guy like this really brought that home. He could accidently step on a rusty nail and feel nothing or even put his hand into a fire I suppose; neither would register with him through pain. It quickly became obvious that as superpowers go this was a double-edged sword as we could take him to the point where things would break or tear and it was only the resistance of the joint itself that made it clear he was about to sustain injury. It meant people had to be incredibly careful working with him.

He explained to me later how the classes had helped him in those dark times and were a lifeline for him going the mental struggles he faced. I cannot even begin to imagine what it would be like to go through all of that, but I do know that he helped me massively to see the martial arts I teach in a different way, and to realise that the human spirit is much stronger than we give it credit for.

The mighty oak v's the spider monkey.

Arak stood six four and over twenty stone. The muscles pushed out from his imposing frame, swollen from a serious amount of time lifting weights. Veins ran close to the surface of the skin and zigzagged up his forearms like tramlines. He was Eastern European and made his living as a nightclub bouncer. He would take pre-training pills, vitamin pills, protein shakes and supplements and I have no doubt he was jacked with enough steroids to turn a donkey into a thoroughbred.

He was gorilla-strong and had that dour, no-nonsense demeanour that a lot of guys from that part of the world have. Occasionally there would be a chink and a sparkle of humour would get through, but that was guarded and kept for a very select few.

At the time I was running classes out of a gym in Bristol and we used to do a Saturday afternoon class. As mentioned above, this was full of bouncers and doorstaff, almost all big men that wanted to mix it up and push the limits. Hardcore would be a reasonable description. As I was working the doors myself it was natural to want to make the training as 'real' as possible due to the nature of the job. So, Saturday afternoons would see us come together and test what we thought we knew.

We had another guy join us along the way. He was also a bouncer, but Arak's polar opposite in build. Hailing from Russia I think, he was small, maybe five eight and no more than twelve stone on a good day. He loved to grapple and had been training in MMA and BJJ for a while. He was a fun addition to the group as we were about to find out.

It was sparring time and the testosterone in the room was so high it was sloshing against the windows and leaking out to the street below.

Arak the mighty oak was about to face the Russian. MMA gloves on and gumshield in, he advanced and started to circle the smaller man. It looked like the mismatch of the century. As our arena was not sport, and weight divisions didn't exist for us, we would mix it up with everyone big or small. Each presented their own set of problems and puzzle to solve.

Arak threw a few very sloppy jabs, confident in his size to win the day; the Russian easily avoided the strikes and hot-footed it back out of range. They danced momentarily before Arak stepped into a strike and overcommitted. The smaller man seeing the opportunity slipped to the side and manoeuvred around him, taking a standing back mount. Like a spider monkey he clambered up the bigger man and clinched in a rear naked choke. Flailing his arms to no avail, the mighty oak slowly began to topple. Clawing at the arm around his neck his knees buckled, he slowly sank to the floor with the Russian clinging to him as a limpet would to a rock.

Making a difference.

One of my students' mums had popped into the club. 'He hasn't hit me since he started training with you'. I took a moment to process that sentence. We were sat at one of the tables in the viewing area with a coffee in hand. I hadn't seen her in over six months; in fact, the last time had been the initial meeting to see if I could help her son. She had phoned me first and outlined the situation which had then led to a meeting where she explained the situation more fully. Her son was in his twenties and had some pretty serious mental health issues. He had always had problems with anger and coping with problems. She wanted to know if I could help. I answered as honestly as I could and explained that martial arts can be beneficial for all sorts of reasons and it could be the case for her son. I went on to say there were no guarantees and not everyone responded positively to the training, but I was prepared to give it a try.

Months went by and he trained weekly with me. The improvement in his physical understanding of the skills was rapid, although we did hit a few stumbling blocks regarding his behaviours and what was acceptable. As I am not an expert in mental health issues, I was aware I could make the situation worse, but I was also aware that the rules and standards of the club needed to be enforced. I decided to give as few concessions as possible to his conditions and when it came time to grade, he was expected to do just the same as everyone else.

Now sat with Mum I knew my gut instinct had been the right choice. Cradling the mug in both hands with slow tears running down her cheeks she thanked me for all the work we had done. She explained that throughout his life he'd had rages and violent outbursts. He had never controlled them and would lash out at everyone, especially Mum. She stood just over five foot and was in later middle age, certainly no match physically for her twenty-something son who towered over her by a foot. She lived in constant fear of these episodes as there was no way to predict them. Saying no to him for something was an obvious one, but a broken biscuit in the pack or the end of a favoured TV show could also trigger violence where he would lash out. It had been that way for over twenty years, and they had lived like that for all that time. A Dad was never mentioned and I can only assume he had been out of the picture for a very long time by the way she talked of her son's childhood.

She spoke quietly gazing into the coffee as she spoke of this, but then lifted her eyes to stare directly at me. 'He hasn't hit me in over six months. He still lashes out and punches walls and doors; he even pushed the television over once when the presenter said something her disagreed with. But he hasn't laid a hand on me since. Thank you, Thank you so much'. Her eyes went back to her coffee as a long, shivering sigh left her lips.

That sentence hit me like a physical blow. This poor women was afraid of her own son and what he might do to her. Once again, I was amazed at what a positive influence martial arts could be, but I was also amazed that he could change the behaviours of a lifetime in a few short months.

22, WHY THE DOORS?

I talk about my time working on the doors in my book, *Modern Samurai; a revealing look into the world of the private security industry.* So if you want to learn more about my time as a bouncer, bodyguard, debt collector and more then take a look.

I had been practising martial arts for a while and like a lot of other young men I was full of ego, pride and curiosity. This created a potent mix of temptations in my young brain. Imagine owning a shiny, red sports car with dream handling and a 0-60 time that would snap your head back, then imagine being told you could sit in it but never drive it. That's how I was feeling. I am in no way comparing myself to a Ferrari, however as a young man with a few years' training in I felt strong and capable, and like most young men I wanted to push the boundaries and see where that would take me.

My first option was competition.

This was an avenue I explored but it didn't answer my questions. The sanitised rule-based variations of fighting never were actually fighting.

Watching people score a point just made the feeling of pretend even more raw for me. I am certainly not dismissing the skill involved in competitive fighting, as having competed in a number of formats I am fully aware of the dedication and sacrifice required to get to the top. MMA, Thai, Judo all are very tough sports where the participants are incredible athletes. Points fighting demands a speed and agility that is lightning fast, and the anaconda style grappling of BJJ means if they get their hands on you it's mostly just a matter of time.

I often say to people that competitive fighting is harder than any other pursuit. I don't know if that's really true, but take a tennis player or a rally driver and see how well their skillset holds up when someone is repeatedly punching them in the face.

The next option was to just go out and pick fights. That would be easy as being socially awkward I always found myself saying the wrong thing anyway. All I needed to do was add a layer of aggression and hey presto, fights would fall in my lap.

My father was known locally as a hard man and had a reputation of a fighter with prowess. He stood six three with a big frame. He was out of shape as a smoker, and the belly overhanging his waist gave away the fact that he was partial to a pint or three. But he was quick, and when he decided to go his actions were fast and decisive. I saw this first-hand on a number of occasions growing up. Here's just one example, and even today all these years after he passed away people still stop me and regale me with past fights my Dad was in. I don't know why they do this, as I do not find any glory in the fact he had hurt people.

I was a kid around eleven or twelve years of age. At that time we lived in a very modest three bedroomed house. It had connecting homes either side and small square garden plots front and back. The back door opened onto a small patio area that had some stepping stones leading off up the small garden to the back gate. Separating us from our neighbours on either side were five foot fences with wooden posts, with those green wire chain links set into diamond patterns between each one.

The afternoon was sunny and as the sun started to pass the tops of the buildings a shadow began to creep across the patio. I was happily playing by myself. I can't recall exactly what I was doing but I do remember something hitting me on my back. I looked around to see no one there. I tried to forget it and carry on when another object bounced off my head. This time I heard sniggering and glimpsed a head as it pulled back inside the upstairs bedroom window of my neighbours' house. I hoped that would be the last of it but no; seconds later another projectile impacted. I looked down to see a clothes peg spin to a stop on the floor in front of me. Annoyed, I picked it up and threw it with all my might towards the open window of my neighbour. All I could hear was laughing and swearing coming from inside.

My dad had heard the commotion and came out wanting to see what was up, just in time to see a head and arm appear out of the window and another peg sail our way. I explained that a few had been thrown and they thought it was funny. Dad decided to articulate his displeasure which was greeted by the words, 'Fuck off,' and other similar expletives.

It turned out next door had sons in their mid-twenties who were visiting. They thought it would be fun to throw things at the kid next door. They also thought they would get away with it. After yelling a bit of abuse through the window, the one brother was dumb enough to come outside. He came out of his back door and was pointing at my dad while shouting. This was a really stupid idea.

My dad, all six three of him, vaulted the fence, grabbed the neighbour by the scruff of the neck and headbutted him. His head shot back and smashed into the wall of the house. He was instantly unconscious and slid down the wall to lie in an untidy heap at the feet of my enraged father. Brother number two had totally lost his bollocks and was refusing to come out of the house. The leap of the fence, clearing the eight to ten feet of garden to get to him and the strike itself were all done in what appeared to be the blink of an eye. The neighbour was out before he realised what was coming. He thought he could stand over there and mouth off and nothing would happen.

Dad went to court over that, as the pathetic cowards who liked to wind up small kids weren't even man enough to accept they deserved what they got and had to go whining to the police. Now as I didn't want to end up in prison street-fighting seemed to be a bad idea. Also morally it was not something I wanted to do. My instructors had rightly instilled in me a belief that these skills should not be used for harm. To intentionally hurt someone or to pick a fight with an innocent party went against everything I had been taught.

This left the doors.

The opportunity arose to work a shift as a bouncer, and I took it. This led to more work, which led to other venues, which led to bigger teams, which led to longer hours, which led to lifestyle choices, which led to a total immersion in the culture of the bouncer.

You might think that being a bouncer or nightclub doorman is the role of a thug or bully, but you would be wrong. Yes, there are unfortunately a few unsavoury types in this field just as there are rotten apples in every barrel. The small percentage that take on this role for those reasons often don't last long and quite often come unstuck. Whether that's by meeting someone better than themselves who gives them the hiding they liked to hand out to others, or the very real threat of legal implications where prison awaits the overzealous doorman.

Most of the role is managing people under stress. Violence, drugs, alcohol, sex, crime. They all live large in the night-time economy and swimming in those waters means you'd better learn to handle conflict. Dealing with people is not something that ever came naturally to me as I have always preferred my own company and find it very hard to deal with people I dislike, which used to be almost everyone. But for some reason I was good at this; not only did I have a certain amount of physical ability, but I could think on my feet and problem solve in the moment. It turned out that dealing with drunk and violent people was something I appeared born to do.

It also gave me the chance to test what I thought I knew and to put to the fire my perceived knowledge. Years of training and never questioning; years of just doing the technique with the promise of understanding and enlightenment somewhere in the distant future would be held accountable right now. Not ten years from now, and certainly not art for art's sake. On a Saturday night at one am when the punters are full of booze and coke, you'd better hope the martial kicks in with your martial art, as matey boy off the local council estate doesn't give a flying fuck if you are a third generation student from some ancient battlefield art that has a rich heritage and lineage dating back centuries. He will push the jagged edge of that broken bottle into your face if you do not physically overpower him and stop him. It is that raw.

I often hear martial arts instructors try to demean door work and the experience it gives you. Mostly these naysayers couldn't fight sleep outside of their own fantasy in the safety of the dojo, but occasionally this opinion is aired through ignorance rather than an inability to see personal weakness. I can only speak for myself when I say this, but my time working did nothing but enhance my knowledge, focus my practice, and prove to me in the now what did and didn't work. The consequences of getting it wrong were very real, and every time you did, someone got hurt. It is that black and white.

I learned how to manipulate people and coerce people to do what I wanted them to do. I learned how to use fear and adrenaline as a weapon. I learned to understand the pantomime of violence and the psychological build-up to violence. I learned to turn it on and off. I came to understand that fights are won and lost very often before a punch is thrown. I learnt how to quiet the mind and how to use body language and gestures to subconsciously guide another's actions. You can talk about this all day long, or read books on the topic, maybe even watch clips on YouTube. None of that will give you a true understanding of how all this works. Only doing it will give you a real, deep understanding of it. And this is where door work has its strength, and why I believe it is incredibly relevant to the conversation of *what do you really know*.

Physically the doors were a fantastic proving ground for your technique. You dealt with whoever was in front of you. No weight categories, no rules and none of them held any respect for your rank or style. If you had a cold or felt a little under the weather, you couldn't pull out of the fight or reschedule. If you had been working sixteen hours straight and not sat down or eaten in over ten it didn't matter. Quite often you would have to deal with numbers and weapons, often dealing with people with a history of serious violence or criminality. There were no referees or tapouts, only the cold reality of a society that has lost its moral compass and would stamp on your head repeatedly if you went down, or the black and white executioner of CCTV which would second-guess you into a prison sentence when viewed by people who do not understand violence but wield the authority of the courts. Every night offered the opportunity where serious violence could explode at any moment and it was our job to deal with that.

23, TEACHING SECURITY.

After working the doors for a number of years I decided to take the plunge and make the investment to become a licensed trainer. This would give me the ability to train door supervisors and help them to gain the qualifications needed to apply for their Security Industry Authority (SIA) license. The SIA is the overseeing body for the industry, and you require a license from it to work in certain job roles.

The Train the Trainer course was an eye-opener in a number of ways for me, as not only did it show me how to deliver the course content but also to understand a lot more about the mechanics of teaching.

Here is where I first learned of a thing called the Competency Ladder, and oh boy, it applied to me. I see it regularly in martial arts instructors up and down the land when teaching outside of their field of expertise. They don't even know they don't know.

The premise of the competency ladder is as follows:

1. You don't know you don't know. Unconscious incompetence.

Example: Think of all the things you had no idea about before you learned to drive.

2. You know that you don't know. Conscious incompetence.

Example: First lesson and you are made aware of all the things you need to know but don't.

3. You know, but have to concentrate on it. Conscious competence.

Example: You drive along at ten miles an hour trying to coordinate your gear changes and learn the road signs.

4. You know, and can perform the task with ease. Unconscious competence.

Example: How you drive now. Putting on your lippy in the rear view, and twiddling with the radio.

Over the years I have had martial artists of all levels on my security courses, from the 7th dan school owner, to the world champion grappler, to the MMA guys through to the very traditional practitioners of the arts. And it always amazed me that all would claim to teach or have been taught self-defence, yet almost without exception they would not even know that they didn't know some of the things they didn't know.

The course itself was split into sections. The first section was how to teach. Up until this point I had been teaching parrot-fashion and really just copying my old instructors' methodology of teaching. I had many lightbulb moments over those few days, as every so often a nugget of information would be shared with the group, and with an ever-growing understanding I could now see why we taught the way we did. Being made aware of the styles of learning and how people absorb information. Learning how to structure your methods to include all of these and finding ways to communicate understanding effectively. For any instructors reading this I would seriously recommend doing a teaching qualification. For me it was one of the most helpful things I have done and really opened my eyes as to why we do what we do.

Then we moved on to the conflict management portion. For years I had been managing people in conflict situations. My understanding thus far on the subject had been instinctive. It had been my role for many years to deal with conflict on the front line at three am in the morning with drunks, druggies and wannabe gangsters. Here you learned your craft; when people say bouncers are bullies and thugs, they don't see the hundreds if not thousands of situations talked down or managed with soft skills every night of the week. We don't get paid to fight; there is no bonus for knocking the punters out and with the ever-increasing eyes of smart phones and CCTV only a fool would rise to violence unnecessarily. The aim is that everyone in the club goes home after enjoying a good night and we the bouncers go home with our shirts intact.

The phrase: *speak softly, but carry a big stick* carries a lot of weight in these environments as the ability to talk down situations is vital, but so is the ability to physically back up what you say if you need to. Over the years I learned the value of understanding the psychology of violence. I call it the fight before the fight. You can find in-depth tutorials on this subject in my Modern Street Systems online courses which can be found here. www.modernsamurai.online

Here in the classroom we learned some of the science behind the actions. I began to get a real appreciation for the nuances of conflict management. So many people get this wrong and misunderstand its value. It's simple really: get this bit right and you won't have to fight.

I think a famous film star and martial artist once stood on a boat and said something similar when asked about his style.

Lastly, we moved into the physical intervention side of the course. This is a very misunderstood area by the martial arts fraternity. The SIA has laid down very specific guidelines as to what the course content will be. This has to be adhered to along with the legal and health implications. Often the criticism of it being of no use is laid at the door of such courses and often martial artists will try to add on all sorts of things to promote their versions. The times I have seen windpipes being 'collapsed', knees and arms being 'snapped' like twigs and chokeholds being 'slammed on' in the name of self-defence while these people totally ignore the legal consequences of their pretend actions. All of these actions if not completely justifiable would land the door supervisor jobless and probably incarcerated.

We were taught low-level restraints and techniques to handle someone who is belligerent but not necessarily violent. In the old days this guy would have got a pasting and been launched down the steps out the fire escape door. Now they are escorted off the premises safely with their dignity intact, even if they don't deserve it.

In the words of Dalton in Roadhouse, 'Be nice, until it's time not to be nice'.

The course was a real learning curve to me which helped my understanding of the martial arts no end. It gave me reasons why we do what we do and a firm understanding of the legalities of our actions. Being armed with this fresh understanding allowed me to go back and revisit all I had learned before and then recategorise and file it in a new order. It also gave me a way to help people to gain qualifications to get a job to feed their families.

Delegates.

We will call this guy Shaun. He had signed up for the Level Two course for door supervisors, and with the other delegates had arrived in the conference room of the chain hotel to be taught. It is always the same on the first day; the chairs and desks are placed in a semi-circle facing my desk. Behind me is a drop-down projector screen where death by PowerPoint awaits them. They slowly file in and as always there are a few stragglers who think punctuality is more of a suggestion than a rule.

As this is happening, I make brief eye contact with people and organise the paperwork. Every so often I tell them I will introduce myself properly when everyone arrives so as not to keep repeating myself. Once everyone is seated, I go through the formalities: breaks, toilets, fire alarms and so on. Then we check ID's and everyone gets prepared for the English assessment. We must do this to make sure everyone has enough grasp of the language to participate fully in the course. I also use this as an opportunity for the delegates to write a little introduction about themselves. I then get them to read this out to the group in a getting-to-know you exercise. It is a way to break the ice while allowing me to gauge both their motivation and level of English. We made our way around the tables in this manner until we reached Shaun.

'Hi, I'm Shaun. I was in the military for a number of years and was medically discharged. I want to get into security to help people and I think the skills I learned in the army will help that'. He spoke confidently and made eye contact with fellow students while making his little speech. I smiled at him and we moved on to the person next to him. Each had a turn and when we had finished, I collected the papers from them, and the course began.

As with all of these courses we had a few smokers on board. You could see them starting to get twitchy as we got nearer to the breaks. When

I announced one, they would leap from their chairs and fast walk down the back stairs, through the lobby and out the sliding doors to the designated smoking areas. Here they would huddle around the overflowing wall mounted ashtrays in all weathers, pulling hard on the first drags to get that all-important nicotine hit.

Shaun was one of these and as I would often join them, we got talking. We were chatting one lunchtime over a takeaway meal deal when he decided to open up to me. The statement he'd given when he introduced himself had been accurate, but now he felt the need to expand on his story. I sat there, sandwich forgotten as he told me of his history.

Shaun joined the military as a young man; swayed by the slick advertising and promise of adventure he had signed up to the infantry. 'To become a grunt,' as he put it. He did his basic training where they taught him how to soldier. Still only a teenager, he was given a weapon and the skills to use it. This was during the time of the Iraq War and Shaun had barely finished basics when he and his fellow infantrymen were loaded onto transport and shipped to the inhospitable world of the army base stationed there. He told me he did three tours in all; each time he watched his mates die and each time fewer came home than went.

I watched his face intently, as you could see his mind going back there behind his eyes. He drew in a deep breath and then slowly let it out. His head dropped as he broke eye contact. 'I have PTSD,' he said. 'It's why I was discharged from the army'. I said nothing, knowing there was more to come and allowing him the freedom to talk at his own pace.

While still looking at the floor he told me that one afternoon they were out. They had contact with the enemy who were entrenched in a village. The fighting was fierce, and an airstrike was called in. The planes came fast, opening up a wave of destruction that decimated the village and everyone in it. When the dust settled, they advanced on the devastation. Buildings had been blown up and the scattered limbs of the villagers lay strewn amongst the debris. Shaun's superiors tasked them with burying the bodies. The remains of women and children were piled with the fighters. Torsos and limbs torn apart in the blast were stacked in a pyre while they dug. Shaun told me that the blood from these children soaked him. His arms were stained red from carrying the mutilated cadavers of the fallen villagers. He told me it had been his 22nd birthday two days before.

Only after telling me this did he look up from the floor. 'I cannot get anything wet on my hands without seeing those babies. Even things like washing up dishes makes me see it like I was there again. Stupid isn't it'. I could think of no words that would offer comfort. The horror of what he said weighed heavy on me and I couldn't believe that after going through such a thing he still wanted to work in a service role helping others. I am pleased to say he passed the course and last I heard was doing well working for a local security firm as a concierge.

Another guy I put through the course I will call Chris.

'I lost my job in management,' he told me. He was a guy in his early fifties, unfit and carrying a lot of excess weight around his beltline. He had studied a very traditional weapon art of Japan many years before, but did no exercise now due to medical issues. He wasn't presenting as the perfect example of a candidate to work as a nightclub doorman.

His ex-company was downsizing, and he was informed he was collateral damage in the changeover. The very next day he assured his wife this would be a short-term issue. Over the breakfast table they had shared through all of his employed life, he now sat buttering his toast with no rush to be anywhere. The commute he took daily on leaving the house at seven forty-five every morning didn't exist, and the office he would have driven to was now inhabited by someone else. Unsure of the appropriate thing to do he had dressed in a shirt and tie that morning as it was a weekday, and they ate breakfast the same time as they always did.

He told me in that first week he applied for over fifty jobs that were management roles in one guise or another. He said he felt confident that his accumulated experience and previous job title would guarantee him a quick release from the purgatory of unemployment. For the first few weeks his resolve held. Even when he heard nothing back from these prospective employers he would still tell his wife that an invitation to interview was just a flap of the letterbox away. But neither postman nor email brought good news and as weeks turned to months Chris began to lose faith. He had been applying for all kinds of jobs and genuinely wanted to work. He had accepted that a downgrade in salary and status would be required, but even then found it hard to find an employer that would give him a try.

A chance meeting with a neighbour had sowed the seeds of an idea in his head. His neighbour was a retired professional who had got bored of the golf, garden centres and allotments of retired life so had returned to join the workforce. He now worked as a security guard for a large car park where he and his colleagues would sit in the security hut and oversee any issues. He worked the night shift and issues were rare so he would spend his evenings enjoying DVDs or a good book. Occasionally he would chat to other workers in the area. It got him out the house and put a few pounds in his pocket.

Chris spent the next morning researching security work, which led to him booking a course, which led to him being sat in front of me. Pencil in hand, shirt and tie on he sat upright and alert, keen to start a new chapter of his life.

It was around four years before I saw him again. One day he just appeared at my gym; he came through the door with his arm outstretched and a big grin on his face. He had lost a little weight since I had last seen him and seemed healthy. It took me a moment to recognise him as it had been a while, by which point he was pumping my hand enthusiastically. He had come in to thank me, and had gone out of his way to do so. He wanted to show me the car he had used to take the journey, so I followed him outside to see a two-year-old mid-range saloon car. I couldn't pretend to be excited about the car until he said it was his new company vehicle, the one he would be driving as he fulfilled his new job role.

After leaving me and finishing the course Chris had gone to work for a company doing static guarding. The pay rate on that was maybe eight pounds an hour and it is a menial role where the majority look down on you. But Chris took the job, grateful to be employed and able to look his wife in the eye again. Over the years he had proved exemplary in the role; punctual and conscientious he made his way through the company until the position he was in today. Last week he had been promoted to area manager for the firm and once again was in a managerial position and able to do the work that he loved to do. He thanked me over and over for helping him to achieve this and would not accept my response that he had achieved this himself.

I do not take any credit for Chris's story, but I do take pride in the fact that I have been able to help people get a job, and better the lives of themselves and their loved ones.

24, THE PUNCH IS ALWAYS THE LAST THING TO GO.

There once was a man who had a past. You could see the clues in his weathered and beaten hands. They were exceptionally large on his frame, rough-skinned and calloused. The knuckles were a spiderweb of scars, and they had been pushed flat to form an anvil of a fist that he had used many times over many years to great effect.

The man you saw now was the husk of what had been, and this was all that was left. I met him when I started to work in a bar in Bristol. He was one of the daytime regulars. He would sit on his stool facing the counter, empty his pockets full of loose change, lint and crumpled bus tickets onto the surface and then patiently count out the exact amount for his pint of beer.

Over the years the drink had overtaken him, and he moved from one day to the next in varying states of disarray. Some days he would be so drunk he would sit in the street outside half-conscious in his own urine; another day would see him pathetically mooching along the kerbside collecting dogends that other people had discarded.

He was actually well liked by the locals despite his poor hygiene and malnourished appearance, and had been around this area for many years now. I was told he was in his seventies and always wore a shabby three-piece suit; it was dirty and frayed and looked older than me. The local café owner would regularly feed him with a large, full English in exchange for some token menial job and he rented a nearby room which he would stumble back to. I do not know where his money came from, but almost every day he scraped together enough to sit on his stool at the bar and sip a few pints to keep the shakes at bay.

And that is where he was sat today. It was late afternoon on a summer's day and the rays of sunlight pierced through the windows creating a natural strobe light effect as they bounced off the rough wooden floor. The room itself was kept dim and cool with tables and chairs scattered around; old-fashioned farming equipment and drawings of Bristol adorned the walls. This was a local bar with a good mix of people which also attracted a number of manual workers who would drop in after work to refresh themselves with a few brews and a game or two of pool.

As it was that time on a Friday afternoon a group of four builder types swung the door heavily against the frame and pushed through the entranceway loudly chatting as they came. Dressed in t-shirts, jeans and work boots with paint-spattered overalls and dirty hands, they made their way to the bar where they loudly shouted for drinks to wash away the sweat of the day. The lads were no different to many others already in the bar apart from the fact no one had seen them before. My guess is they were working nearby but were not from the local area. As they were ordering drinks and making crude comments about the pretty barmaid, they surrounded the old man and jostled him from his stool.

With a laughing apology the builders moved away from the bar, pints in hand to go find the pool table. The old man smiled back and resat himself on the stool. The pretty barmaid reached across the bar towards him, gently tapped the sleeve of his jacket and winked. No real harm had been done, just a couple of rowdy builders unwinding after a hard day's graft onsite in the sun.

The dust of the building site was obviously thick in the mouths of the builders as it was not long before one of the group was back at the bar. As he ordered the round of drinks he looked sideways at the old man and sneered at the vision before him. When the barmaid handed over the drinks the builder said loud enough for everyone to hear, 'What's that dirty old pisshead doing sat there?' As he spoke, he reached a steel toe-capped boot out and clipped the leg of the stool causing it to shake and forcing the old man to nearly spill the drink he was carefully sipping. Once more the old man said nothing. As the builder walked away you could hear him shouting to his group that he hoped he hadn't caught anything from being so close to the old fart.

As it was a glorious summer's evening and the start of the weekend for many, the bar was slowly starting to fill up with work colleagues grabbing a drink and the early party crowd getting a few in before heading to town. The bar area was getting quite cramped with people ordering drinks as the builder returned once more for another round for the boys. He couldn't find an opening and with a twenty-pound note waving in his hand he started to push past the old man to access the bar.

The old man reached a decision in that moment. His patience for the utter disrespect spent, the old man pushed back, forcing the builder to stagger. His large frame wobbled from the force, and as what had happened dawned on him and comprehension sunk in his face scrunched up in a mask of anger. The builder balled a fist and drew back to strike out but was completely unprepared for the swift cross the old man threw as he pushed himself from the stool, transferred all his remaining weight and muscle mass down his arm and threw that meaty hand into the oncoming, unprotected jawline of the builder. His head snapped back as he was spun by the force of the blow. He fell unconscious to the floor; a low moan came from his broken jaw as the amazed punters looked on. The old man turned and apologised to the barmaid, swigged down the last few gulps of his pint and stepped over the sleeping giant. No one moved to interfere or stop him; the other guys in the group were in a moment of disbelief. They had watched it happen but just could not process the information seen with their own eyes.

The old man had been a bare-knuckle fighter. For years he had travelled the country with the fairs taking on all-comers in cash fights where the winner took all. He would often fight three to four times a night with the local hard men and bullies. He had been schooled in the art of pugilism in the rawest way possible and had honed those skills in an unforgiving arena for many years. At night after the shows he and his colleagues would train with whatever equipment they could find and soak their hands in vinegar and horse piss; at least that's what he told me.

The next afternoon he was back on his stool quietly sipping his pint as if nothing had happened.

25, WHAT DOESN'T KILL YOU MAKES YOU STRONGER IS BULLSHIT.

I had been bounced around all day, and now I lay still, stiff as a board. This time I didn't bounce but fell as if shot.

Today's venue was a community centre in Neath, not the most picturesque part of Wales, but we weren't here for the scenery. I'd made the trip up together with a friend called Gavin, who was also an instructor. I had picked him up in a supermarket carpark before the sun had risen fully. It was a grey, wet morning and the rain was monotonous on the windscreen. We whiled away the journey talking about all things martial and before we knew it, we were there. The chequered flag appeared on the sat nav as she announced in her best robotic English,' You have arrived at your destination'. She said nothing about parking though and it took another two laps of the side streets to find a space.

We had driven here as a friend was holding a seminar and a few of the best Judo and Ju jitsu instructors were teaching on it. It was a great opportunity to meet old friends and learn some new tricks. Japanese Ju Jitsu for those that don't know is the core knowledge where Judo and Brazilian Ju jitsu come from. It is a battlefield art that covers all ranges; it's now somewhat overshadowed by its modern-day counterpart, but that doesn't detract from the usefulness of the art. There are many interpretations of Ju jitsu with many styles nuancing a slightly different take, and in this room we were lucky to have some truly knowledgeable instructors from eighth dan to sixth dan black belt.

Gavin my training partner for the day was not small at six three and nineteen stone; he was also not delicate. As a Karate instructor his practice was hard and unyielding, and the flow of the movement was mostly eluding him. Think circles not squares. He could perform the techniques well, but they had a certain rigidity to them that was leaving me rather sore. Joint locks done in this manner are never pleasant and the instructors were showing us the worst of these. Arms and wrists were bent into the most unnatural of shapes as we feigned snapping bits off each other with great enthusiasm.

The room was upstairs and through a door with a portal window. The whole area was matted with a row of old school benches down one side. Windows ran the length of two walls opening out to a view of greyness and rain. I had dusted off my gi for this, as these days I rarely wore one anymore, and was now regretting doing so as this was the thing being used to catapult me into the air to land on my back into the mats.

We had moved onto some throws and the rapid-fire machine-gun style of the instructor was not helpful to those who needed more of a breakdown. He would call out an *uke* (demonstration partner) and show a throw with ferocity and precision. He would also do it at full speed. Then he would quickly break it down once and repeat at half speed, and then you were expected to perform it. He kept a fast pace and was exceptionally knowledgeable. Shortish in stature but with an air of indestructability about him, he ran through his session with a weird mix of humour and very real application, smiling one minute, wide-eyed astonishment the next as he would launch his student at speed to come crashing down to earth. They say there are no strikes in Judo, Others say there are, as you are being hit with a planet. This was a demonstration of this in action. Throw after throw was executed with devastating accuracy and each time the landing seemed incrementally worse than the next. The idea of those impacts on a pavement or concrete floor sent shivers through me.

We had been practising for a few hours now and my body unused to this kind of punishment these days was beginning to resist. This is a bad thing as you need to be loose to take the throw; your body needs to go with the energy so as not to injure yourself. As we progressed, I could feel my body stiffening a little more after each fall. I would get back up and set for another, trying to force myself to relax.

Another instructor had taken the floor by now. Again, shortish with a mischievous glint in his eye (a recurring theme for Japanese Ju jitsu instructors it would seem). You could tell his natural emotion was cheerful, but like the others a rod of steel ran through him and there was no mistaking the very real capabilities of the man.

He is actually a good friend of mine as well, and it is amazing the depth of knowledge he holds. Hailing from up north with a Newcastle type twang but living in darkest Wales he is a conundrum of a personality. Ex-military with a wealth of knowledge on all things martial he is one of the humblest people I know. Of all the martial artists out there shouting about how good they and their style are, few will have the depth of understanding this man has. Incredibly underrated by the martial arts community at large he just smiles and says it's a good thing as he doesn't have to deal with the politics.

Sore, battered, and stiff, the majority of the day was over, but we still had more training to do. This is where listening to your body is a good idea; I didn't. Ego was overruling my decision-making process and the sensible thing to do at this time was to concede. I was a man in my mid-forties carrying a raft of historic injuries from competition and door work, and being honest a little soft on my own training as I was always teaching those days. But instead I let pride interfere. I didn't want to concede any weakness in front of my peers, nor did I want to let my training partner down, so I ignored the many warning signs my body was yelling out at me and continued on.

Grips were established; hand wrapped deep into the lapel of my jacket my opponent shifted his bodyweight and stepped into the throw. Getting low he came under my base and the momentum carried me up into the air and over down towards the mat. I landed wrong; stiff from the day my attempt at a breakfall was insufficient and the impact jarred the wind from my chest as pain shot through me. I lay on my back not moving, staring up at the grubby polystyrene ceiling tiles as I tried to figure out if I should move. I gave myself an experimental wiggle and immediately regretted it as pain coursed through me. It felt like hot molten lava was running down my lower back and the slightest movement magnified it one hundred percent.

People had gathered now and were looking down at my prostrate frame as I laid there unable to move. I have never liked people fussing when I am in pain and this was no exception so the chatter going on overhead was annoying, especially as I couldn't escape it. I lay like that for a few minutes and then stupidly decided to try to move. The pain was bad but as I knew it was coming now was a little easier to manage. I was helped to the side of the mats where I lay back down flat on my back and just like in that scene from *Kill Bill* where the bride wiggles her toes in the back of the pussy wagon pick-up, I did the same. Testing the pain levels of each movement. It hurt a lot, but if I wiggled my toes was that worse or better than if I tried to clench a butt cheek? Raising a heel off the ground was way worse than lifting a hand, and for the time being lifting my shoulders off the floor was too painful to contemplate.

Through stupidity or sheer bloody-mindedness, I made it home. The pain was intense; my movement was incredibly limited and by the next day it had not improved at all. I could walk in a very slow shuffle but could not bend over. Like a Dalek in *Dr Who* stairs were my nemesis and if forced to tackle them it felt like I was trying to summit Everest.

Hold on to the railing with both hands and lift one leg. Use the railings like a tug of war rope to heave my other leg over the lip of the step then stop and breathe as the pain brings out the sweats. Getting in a car was a similar process and lifting myself in and out shot waves of that molten lava through my body, which was a shame; quite a few car journeys were in my immediate future as I had hospitals and doctors to see.

I had ruined the discs in my lower back with that failed landing; the doctors did their tests and booked me in for appointments. X-rays were taken, and physiotherapy began. Months went by and all the while my gym was open, and I was running classes. I would shuffle across the floor like Frankenstein's monster in a slow, painful gait to then explain in a frustrated manner to the student what I wanted as I couldn't show them. For the first time in my life I felt weak and helpless, unsure of the future and utterly fed up with not being able to do what I had always done.

The devil makes work for idle hands, is a well-recognised saying, and between the boredom and the pain I was drinking more than I should. Couple that with the lack of exercise and my weight began to creep up. I was turning into Homer Simpson and there was very little I could do about it. This stage lasted about six months where I was in constant pain and had a very limited range of movement, but slowly things improved little by little. The pain now would ebb and flow like the tides; instead of constant I would now have good and bad days. The good days meant that after all this time I could once again get my left leg to waist height and for a person who could always kick head height no problem that was an achievement. The bad days meant it hurt to move. Every step was like an electric shock and holding the pads in class was agony with every punch that impacted on them.

It was about a year before it had healed enough to start thinking about training again properly. Psychologically it was a big leap as I would need to push myself to get back into shape, but I was scared of going too far and going back to square one. That is not a six months I ever wish to repeat. I still get bad days and as with most people, once you have had a back injury it becomes like that annoying family member who pops up every now and again to remind you that they are still around. Whoever came up with the saying: *What doesn't kill you makes you stronger* never had a back injury as the only thing that got stronger from it was my Chiropractor's bank balance.

26. AN INVITE TO THE DANCE.

We have all heard the phrase: *A big fish in a little pond*, right? Being there is warm, cosy, and reassuring with no pressure to excel or grow. It's comfortable there and as we confidently navigate the familiar waters, we find ourselves stagnating slowly. Going backwards in fact as not moving forward while everyone else does is actually reversing.

This began to change for me when I recently received an invite to sit at the big table. Suddenly I became a very small fish in a very big pond. I had been offered the chance to teach on the biggest stage of the entire UK martial arts scene.

The morning had arrived where I headed off to participate in the UK Martial Arts Show at the Doncaster Dome. I had a teaching slot both days alongside some of the brightest stars in the business. The timetable was jacked with movie stars and top-level names; people who I had read about for years in the magazines would be there as would a room full of my peers and fellow instructors. Everyone who was anyone would be in the venue and all would be expecting the best from everyone involved.

I think it was the fabled wise women Carol Decker from T'Pau who in her vocal teachings once said,

> *Don't push too far your dreams are china in your hand*
>
> *Don't wish too hard, because they may come true and you can't help them*
>
> *You don't know what you might have set upon yourself*
>
> *China in your hand.*

Well here I was, and the dream was real.

I was lying in bed, my eyelids rolled up like shutter blinds at six thirty am. I had no reason to be awake this early as I didn't need to be up for another two hours, but like a kid at Christmas my brain would not let me rest. I lay motionless trying to focus on the swirling patterns above me on the bedroom ceiling as the dawn light entered through the cracks in the curtains. Self-doubt was bouncing around in my head just like a three-year-old on a space hopper, pigtails flapping. Boing! Am I good enough? Boing! Will anyone turn up? Boing! Will too many turn up? Boing! Will someone try to physically challenge me? Boing! What if nobody likes it? With every bright orange bounce of the manically grinning ball my inner voice was telling me to call in sick, make an excuse, invent a dying elderly grandparent, or purposely catch the flu right now.

I lay there and breathed, remembering all the many years of classes that had gone before. I remembered all the students, all the security courses, the military personnel, NHS staff and bailiffs that I had taught, the years spent learning and refining my martial arts knowledge. And finally, I remembered the amazing people who I'd learnt these things from. The knowledge I would be sharing was not mine but borrowed from the vast library of many Sensei and instructors before me. The phrase, *Standing on the shoulders of giants* was very real to me in that moment, and as I relaxed my breathing and started to regulate my inhales and exhales, I quieted the dissent in my mind.

A slow breath in starting low as my belly expanded, moving up to my chest as my lungs filled with morning air, finally absorbing the last of the oxygen as I tried to suck the last bit into my brain. At last I reached a slow count of ten and allowed myself to exhale, in through the nose and out through the mouth. I repeated these thirty times to the slow mantra of *one, two, three*, all the way to ten as my chest rose and fell. I no longer heard the space hopper, instead I saw my future where my seminars were successful, and I performed them with confidence and calm. In fact, I pictured more than that. I saw a virtuoso performance, my own personal equivalent to Freddie Mercury's performance at Live Aid. I saw myself rising to the challenge and smashing it. After all, I'd asked for this. Now the time had come to walk the walk and I knew I could.

With the car loaded I started the drive to Doncaster. It was a three-and-a-half-hour road trip from my house, and I had gotten into the habit of listening to audiobooks on my journeys. Today's offering was the American drawl of Grant Cardone as he told me all about the 10X rule. His excitement was palpable and it was very clear than anyone within one hundred feet of the man would be enthused with the need to achieve greatness. 'Don't be a pussy,' he said while explaining how we should accept responsibility in the distinct dialect of the Louisiana male. The miles of the motorway slid by the windows as I listened with my arse getting number and number at each new set of roadworks. As always there seemed to be an endless stream of cones but workmen were rarer than a yeti in the summertime. Eventually I reached my destination and unfolded out of the car in the shape of a question mark. The years have taken their toll and it now takes ten minutes to stand straight after a long journey. Think of it as a condensed version or the evolution of man, from Neanderthal to homo erectus in minutes rather than millennia.

The show didn't start until the next day but as I pulled up, I saw one of the organisers Bob Sykes in the hotel carpark. We exchanged greetings as he told me he couldn't find the hotel he was meant to be in which was booked by his co-organiser Paul Barnett. I was no help as I didn't know the area so instead, I went to get booked in. Already there were some great people in the hotel reception; a sign of the great weekend to come. The whole weekend was a blur of meet and greets of old friends and new. Being introduced to genuine legends who would mutter, 'I dabble a bit' when questioned through to TV personalities and film stars like Chris Crudelli and Zara Pythian.

As always, the legendary Bill 'Superfoot' Wallace was in attendance and it was a privilege to speak with him again. It is as if Father Time himself is scared of the man, as he never seems to age.

The morning dawned of the opening day of the show. I meet a friend at breakfast who was going to be performing on stage that day and was giving a concise but thorough breakdown of what breakfast components affect chi, and in what way. I must admit to having been invested in my full English so didn't heed the advice. However, it must have worked because he smashed it on stage. He went up alone onto a platform designed for group demos and captivated the audience with a display of Tai Chi that was both beautiful and powerful at the same time. It was great to see both the demonstration and the genuine pleasure he got from doing it. Well done Andrew.

My time had come. I had been hiding my nerves throughout the day and taking in the events around me. The hall was set out into zones which were surrounded by stalls around the perimeter; at one end was the largest area that would house the most popular workshops, at the other end was the main stage. I was on zone two. The area was ringed off with portable metal railings that stood on a roughly laid grey industrial carpet. Thoroughfares ran around and through the zones and people were milling about as the distorted sound of the announcer cut across the hum of the many conversations being had, and I made my way to my area. A class was already running as I set up my second-hand Canon 600 to record the session. Tripod extended and lens cap off I pointlessly fiddled with the camera to kill time and give myself something to do. The session before came to an end, and I stood there alone in a sea of dirty grey as not one single person joined us. My worst fears were coming to fruition and I sat there, self-consciously talking to a friend as I felt more and more embarrassed at the complete no-show of people. What should I do at this point? Now I understood why everyone brings students. This would be a hard lesson learned, but just as I was about to slink off and my friend had run out of conciliatory noises a mini miracle happened. People started to arrive.

It seems we are never too old to learn a lesson and I was humbled and so very grateful to see familiar faces and new ones come forward to join my class. The timetable of the zones had an overlap and people had been finishing on other areas before they could join me. As they arrived, I gratefully shook hands with as many as I could and started to teach.

I had a lot of fun with the class and after the initial hiccup soon found my stride and ploughed into the task at hand. I partially strangled a world champion in my enthusiasm and dumped black belts on their arses. I also got students from many disciplines to adopt my way of moving while explaining why I do things the way I do. The whole session was topped off with a group photo full of smiling people who had enjoyed the workshop and gained from it.

A few mornings later I received this message:

Many thanks, I would like to bring you here for courses in the future. Having looked around the room at the weekend you would certainly be my first choice for effective self-defence.

It was great to receive such high praise although being truthful far more than I deserved or warranted given the amazing talent that was in the room. But I took his kind words as a positive moving forward and used them as a sign that I did ok.

27. WHY DO WOMEN SHAVE THEIR EYEBROWS OFF ONLY TO DRAW THEM ON AGAIN?

It was a Friday night and I was working the shift as a doorman. Tonight, was a little different as it was the *Children in Need* appeal the BBC do every year. The wonderful event where millionaire tax dodgers implore us to dig deep and spare a few quid. So, I was forced to endure that one-eyed bear and countless unfunny celebrities doing totally unfunny stuff. Couple that with the group of personalities who were off on an all-expenses paid jolly in the name of the poor little children playing across all the big screens in the bar and my night was not shaping up to be great.

As someone who doesn't watch television, I despise the BBC with a depth of loathing that I believe is well founded. The annual mugging of the license fee so they can keep brainwashing the masses with biased reporting even though I use none of their services is nothing short of theft with menaces. But here it was, and the bar and its inhabitants were taking part.

This was a local suburban sports bar that boasted the pint glass emblem in the corner of the big screens so people could get their footy fix. The bar offered microwaved pub grub, with a clientele to match. Mostly working class and firmly entrenched in the ritual of a Friday night down the local, they congregated along the bar and around the pool tables. Apart from a few idiots the majority were friendly, and I had built up a good rapport with staff and punters alike in the time I had been working there. Every Friday and Saturday the license said they would need two door staff and I was one of them. Mostly we would stand at the door with the occasional walk around to make sure everyone was playing nicely. Tonight turned out to be a little different.

Some of the locals and staff had organised a few fundraising ideas and were rattling the buckets they had, egged on by the famous faces on the screen. As the night wore on the laughter became more raucous as the drinks started to flow and the suggestions to make a few extra pounds became more outlandish. One of the barmaids came over and came up with the suggestion that I should have my legs waxed for charity. It turns out that the pub was awash with wannabe beauticians and there was no shortage of willing volunteers to take part in the deed. I smiled and refused, but like a dog with a bone they weren't going to leave the idea alone. They harangued me repeatedly until I managed to convince them of a compromise: if they could raise £100 in sponsorship, I would allow them to wax my eyebrows.

To my utter dismay the money was raised in minutes and a chair was brought forth to be placed smack bang in the middle of the bar area for all to see. The stage was set and all that was needed now was my stupid butt on the chair. I took a seat as one of the jean-clad young barmaids straddled my leg and brought her face close to mine, peering at me intently. A crowd was gathering, and it seemed the punters wanted their money's worth as they had formed a ring around myself and the two barmaids who were performing the task.

I was aware there would be sticky strips involved and hot wax, but I didn't know that cheering mixed with *ooohs* and *aaahs* were part of the deal. I won't pretend that I sat stoically unmoving as they dehaired my face as I didn't. It bloody hurt and left angry red welts where my eyebrows once were. These now sat attached to the strips of tape which the barmaids were waving around in some sort of victory dance. Moment over, the crowds went back to drinking and playing pool and I went back to my door with a new problem to work out.

I was just a few days away from my Mum getting remarried and I was to give her away. I had no idea how much of an impact it makes to the look of your face to suddenly have angry red stripes where eyebrows once lived and now as I looked at my reflection in the mirror I was left with the question. Should I leave them as they were, or like a lot of ladies, should I try to draw false ones on like McDonald's golden arches . . . ?

A real fighter.

It is a real privilege to be able to help people and running the club allows us to do exactly that. We raise funds twice a year for local good causes and this time we had chosen a local young lady who had been afflicted with cancer.

Jessica was a vibrant, beautiful fourteen-year-old girl who despite this horrible disease refused to be anything other than positive. How she maintained such an upbeat manner at that time was beyond me, as unfortunately the treatment was taking its toll. The regular doses of chemotherapy that were being used to fight the cancer made Jessica feel very weak, but much worse than that for a teenage girl it also made her hair fall out. After hearing her story and learning that one of the things she really wanted was a decent wig I knew the wonderful members at our club could help.

The NHS is a fantastic organisation staffed by incredible people and they had been amazing in the treatment of Jessica. However, they are straining under continued cuts to funding and an ever-ageing population and budgeting the finances has become a real tightrope for the bean counters. One of the ways they had managed to save a few pounds was to supply the patients with very cheap, nasty wigs made with fake hair.

This to Jessica was a step too far. The chemo, the illness, the time off school and the endless hours in hospital waiting rooms away from friends were one thing, but bad hair was entirely another. So, the idea was to fundraise to pay for a wig made of real human hair which it turned out was quite expensive.

I rallied the parents and students and we brainstormed what we could do to raise money. All the usual ideas were thrown around and dismissed when someone mentioned a charity walk. Then someone else suggested using the phrase: *Walk a mile in my shoes*, which seemed to hold some power in the message. Then it was suggested that a mile was not far so we would need to jazz it up. Instantly it was suggested that myself and some of our male instructor team don high heels and totter the mile, gouging blisters the size of dinner plates into our heels as we went. It seemed to be a great revenge for the years of press-ups we had communally handed out in the eyes of the students. We hurriedly dismissed this and explained it was meant to be fun, which fortunately the team accepted so we moved onto some other suggestions.

The day of the walk arrived, and it was great to see so many of the club come together like this. We met outside the front of the gym and we took turns admiring each other's outfits. Some had gone for silly shoes while others had gone for the full fancy dress. One of the girls had jelly-filled wellies, and one of the boys was dressed as Iron Man while a father and son team turned up in fully inflated sumo suits, which created a good laugh from everyone. I was wearing giant furry monster slippers with claws coming out the end that the dog was desperately trying to attack. This proved a little awkward on the walk as he fixated on getting to my feet, and at nine stone he usually gets what he wants. Around forty of us had made the effort and some had brought their dogs along, so we looked like a motley bunch as we made our way down the road to follow the designated route that was exactly one mile. I had arranged it so we passed a park half-way and the kids ended up fighting with the sumo guys as to who would get to go on the swings.

Walk over we tallied up the sponsorship money and to the delight of everyone we had smashed our target and raised over eight hundred pounds. Handing the money over to Jessica was a great moment, but an even greater moment was to come. Soon after we learned that the chemotherapy had worked, and she had been given the all clear which was amazing as she and her family had fought it so hard. Jessica remains cancer free.

A great idea is born.

Recently I was approached by a man named John. One of Geoff Thompson's former students who runs a small club outside of London they have christened *Bastard Hybrid No Name Wrestling*, or something like that, he stands six three with strong shoulders. Even in his early seventies he is very physical. This is counterbalanced by a softly spoken voice with an artistic and friendly demeanour. Don't phone him unless you have at least an hour spare as he loves a good chat and will talk to you barely drawing breath about the most random subjects. Although time-consuming he is always entertaining.

He contacted me with an idea he had been kicking around for a number of years. The aim was to find a way to help veterans struggling with PTSD, mental illness, homelessness and substance abuse. He suggested allowing a few of these guys to come and train at his club for free, but I had bigger ideas. Due to being lucky enough to be around some incredibly talented people who go out and get shit done my own dreams and aspirations were growing too. In a fit of colossal overenthusiasm I told John that we could make this national, maybe even global, and help thousands of people along the way. I had zero idea of how we were going to achieve this and history books one day will report if we did.

Team Fightback was born in that moment. I was walking across a local farmer's field; my dog was chopping between sniffing the doggie news in the hedgerows and belting across the field as fast as he could run. The sun was up and with little cloud cover a warm breeze swayed the treetops. 'John,' I said, 'how about if we make it so clubs from all over the country can join and create training space nationally for these guys to access martial arts? Let's create programmes where we can train them to be instructors and earn a living for themselves. Let's give them all the tools required to run a business'. I couldn't see John's face at that point but in the silence that followed my outburst I pictured him with eyes wide and a slightly shocked expression on his face. To his credit he barely skipped a beat. 'Let's do it,' he said.

We put together a basic outline of how we were going to achieve this, ninety percent of which was nothing more than ideas with no substance and no access to the knowledge required to get there. But then the most amazing thing happened. People started to gravitate towards us and the project. We had been in talks with Combat Stress for a while and it was going nowhere. We needed a partner with the knowledge and experience to do some real good, and we found Minds at War; a group of very dedicated people doing great things right now - exactly who we needed working with us. We needed a website; no problem, the country's leader in online martial arts donated his time to us for free. We needed some infrastructure for members; again, no problem as a wonderful lady got in touch and gifted her software to the cause. But what about setting up the structure legally and starting to look for funding? Once again the universe provided us with the right person. So many great people are already on board and we are still at the embryonic stage of what I am sure will be an amazing project. We still have a very long way to go and many obstacles to overcome, but with such amazing people joining us we cannot fail.

Please take a minute and check out www.teamfightback.org when you can and join us to help to make a real difference.

Printed in Poland
by Amazon Fulfillment
Poland Sp. z o.o., Wrocław